A Choir of Honest Killers

☙

by Buddy Wakefield

Write Bloody Publishing

writebloody.com

First edition.
ISBN: 978-1949342017

Cover Design by Tim W. Sanders
Cover Photograph by Roger Ballen
Interior Layout by Winona León
Proofread by Aly Sarafa and Dan Steinbacher
Author Photo by Asia Samson

Edited by Derrick C. Brown, Anna Freeman, Keaton Maddox, Aly Sarafa, Veronika Shulman, Alyesha Wise, and Scott Woods

Type set in Bergamo from www.theleagueofmoveabletype.com

Printed in the USA

Write Bloody Publishing
Los Angeles, CA

Support Independent Presses
writebloody.com

Dedicated to awful men.

A Choir of Honest Killers

A Choir of Honest Killers

In the dream I was allowed to ask any question
so I asked how many deaths I was responsible for
and the voice said *All of them.*
Did I save any lives?
All of them.
How many lives will I live?
All of them.

MADE IT BIG
December 25, 2016

In seventh grade, I prayed for wisdom while taking a shit and crying about how much pain I was in for wanting a man to live in my body instead of the suffering and the puppy and the girl who did. My body lived in Baytown, Texas. The old end of Country Club. A bike ride away from a dead strip mall, humid on the blacktop, holes in that. "Praying for Time" by George Michael is still the soundtrack for the first time I asked an idol for wisdom. Jesus Christ.

What a year. We get it. People hated 2016. Even though they sidled up to the tragedy every chance they got. Me? Surprised myself. Didn't give much energy to it. Detached. I got respect for all them who passed. Harper Lee. Prince. David Bowie. Leonard Cohen. Especially Leonard. Remove my hat and watch my head tilt, Muhammad Ali. Gene Wilder. Merle Haggard. Didn't even let the death of the American presidency press me to comment. If death is what the collective conscious needs to gain consciousness, bring it. But I did feel the wind leave my body for a minute when George Michael died tonight.

Wasn't all that femininity he had to wear, how it looked like the same reason I got called a fag every day for the way I walked and talked and the interests I had back then, way before I wanted anyone to know they were right about me. It wasn't how happy George Michael made my mom with his song at the skate rink. Wasn't his whole catalogue. Because it wasn't.

Was the way he'd stolen from the radio down to my tape deck, then into the cassette player in the bathroom, then sang "Praying for Time" while I was on the toilet taking a shit and begging God to give me so much wisdom I couldn't ever be sad again.

HARMONY ENEMY

Everybody's got a story that comes from an awful story

that lives inside a story that's dead.

Stop telling it. Perfect

probably isn't what you think it is.

What are we even aiming at when we use that word?

There will be a lot of shooting.

Most of it won't be straight.

Don't worry.

You don't have to be good at everything.

There are so many people here.

If you really want to do something flawless,

stay present. Your fate

is just another word for now, just another name for

transmute density.

Meditation is critical. And mercy. Have mercy.

These bodies are a sticky hologram.

Being human does not require any further context.

Your expectations of me are not my responsibility.

Those are yours. Everyone

gets the same amount of time to live their lives.

I want to be a reliable narrator for a living,

so I'll just tell you the worst of it first

and be done with it.

Realizing the transparency of my neediness

was dignity well spent.

Forgiveness is a matter of advocating for dignity.

When my body came home from the shame experiment,

the first thing I saw was its resolve.

If you still aren't willing to cut every loss,

you are not yet prepared to qualify.

Cut the loss. The story of it. I stopped being nostalgic

when I started keeping up.

Seeing a man run as fast as he can

still gives me goosebumps.

I'm not scared to die, I just don't want it to hurt.

I bet the biggest misconception about death

is that we won't care anymore.

I will never not love you.

Hiding the absence of your love is a

mathematical impossibility.

You were the year I wished my life on other people.

Magnets are incapable of lying.

Perfect was incapable of telling the truth.

Darkness is redundant. I wanted us to be the truth.

I meant to do it correctly.

In loving gain of our memory. And mercy.

Have mercy.

Do not flake on the blessing.

There is every such thing. We were every such thing.

I may have been grossly underprepared to receive love.

Was it even in this lifetime that we knew each other?

Tonight, I painted my apartment

and remembered every life I've ever lived,

including the one where you read this.

Was I really too sensitive,

or were you just too unconscious?

And if you weren't too unconscious,

then were you just being cruel?

Maybe we work our way to the middle.

Maybe we work our way into what we are.

Why don't you want to know what we are?

I'll cut your costume loose. Cut you right out of it.

When something is absent, it is absolutely

not in your way. Get in my way.

Come remind me what we are together. Do it soon.

Soon we will have to say what we have to say

to each other's faces.

Mine is *I love you*. Mine is *Have mercy*.

I just wanted to throw something as hard as I could.

I wasn't paying attention

to what it would do when it landed.

Strawberry

My first memory is of the first time I saw the sky.
Epic reckonings are often benign, so don't worry,
I'm just a letter in an envelope
as far as the ocean above us is concerned.

What led to the second thing I remember about
this life was being terrified out of my sky story
and into the events that follow,
until I woke up in an octopus.

This is a true story, a brief history of my best guess
at what my body has been calling sex.

My second memory was at a stoplight. I was three.
Mom assures me that we were not at a stoplight, that we were in
motion, driving on the 610 Loop,
and that I was actually eight.

It is no small wonder how I managed to confuse a stoplight with a
loop that literally encircles the entire city of Houston, or that there's
a five-year differential between my actual second memory and what I
believed to be my second memory.

I am not light reading. There is no pause button. Absorb what you
can. Add it up later. This is not the time for pretending we can't hear
Chechnya raping that woman in the first *Mad Max* movie, terrorizing
a mother and her baby. Killing them.

I hope Mel Gibson's heart has learned to risk more softness. I hope
his attackers have too. If you really wanna understand what I've
come here to say, then you have to remember—there's a point of
connection in everything. My nickname for God is The Math.

The Math is a word problem.

In 1982, a red pickup truck pulled up next to my mother on the 610
Loop. In the bed of it was an upright, strapped-in motorcycle with a
strawberry-blonde bearded drunk riding high and unbathed in the seat.

Only a woman could have given a man like that his
strawberry color. Only women have the guts to give
birth to men. There are *a lot* of people in this world already aware of
what I am just now finding out. There are no stoplights on
the 610 Loop.

Mom says there was no such thing as a man sitting on a bike in the
bed of that truck, said, *There was a truck with a motorcycle in it, yes, but
there wadn't no Strawberry.* She did say though,
that four men on motorcycles were riding right behind it.

I don't remember that. I don't remember how many tentacles it had.
But I do remember what I dreamed after seeing *Mad Max*, how The
Acolytes yanked my mother through the car window, bashed her up
to blood in the dust. Laughed about it.

Me in the back seat, shrunk to the size of a tadpole, in the
sunken-eyed section of a nightmare, knowing that giving myself to
violent men would be the only protection a three-year-old could
offer, to give them what they wanted. Something soft.

Don't talk to me about what it means to petrify until you've lived at a
stoplight, unless you've dreamed your worst death and believed it was
about to happen. I remember Strawberry leaning on down to look at
Mom, a sloppy laughing inquiry

into her lap, her driver's seat. A slug

is the closest known land relative to the octopus. Octopodes
communicate neurologically. Felt to me like Strawberry wanted to
party. Felt like his fun, grizzly buddies in the cab did too, smiling the
way a follower smiles. The way drunk soldiers smile. The way men
with no Math smile.

Wanted to throw things around a little. Wanted to slap a knee about
it. Or an ass. Grab some titties. Grab the softness off. Eat a gazelle.
Chase it down first. They laughed. And they laughed. Hyenas. They
could take what they want if they wanted.

There are too many moral people, noble people, whom I admire, who might come to see me as disgusting if they find out my behavior, how my body copes with sex. How strong humiliation makes me. Three-year-olds don't get credit for learning survival like this.

You've probably already forgotten that when an eight-year-old boy feels too much pressure to be a man, he will remember his body as three just to dismantle the shame of himself. Even when he's forty-four.

I don't know how to stalk things. If that's what being a man is, I never was one. I was working to figure the difference between safety and the long walk home. Was trying to outrun my faggot before it could make me any softer.

Was bearing the weight of watching my heroes believe I would burn forever, and loving them anyway. This is what I know about being a man. Straight people need a gun for power like this. Y'all look like Russia, hiding behind his dumb Chechen son.

My mama played her best southern bell for those bikers, played her kindness, played it well, knew that fear only speeds up chaos, so she just smiled and pointed to her three-year-old son in the passenger's seat having his second memory. I was at a stoplight.

They were all in motion on the 610 Loop.

When we finally pulled away, I was eight, sobbing and incompetent. The only way an eight-year-old can protect his mother from a blur of men is to give them what they want. Nurture. My nature.

Stop trying to figure it out. I done told you, boy.
I am a woman from the bottom of a food chain living in the body of a man at the top. A letter in an envelope. The first time I saw the sky. Put here to stop giving birth to the apocalypse.

I still don't know why—when presented with the opportunity to invent an alternative reality—some writers go to such great lengths to make us worse than we already are. In 1979, *Mad Max* was released, a gang of bikers tormenting strangers.

It didn't even have to exist. Chechnya doesn't even have to exist. They are certain I don't. If men stop cultivating a fear of death, does the apocalypse lose its charm? Does everybody soften up? Please, use your words or go back underwater.

I know you're petrified about feeling useless, about what to do with your power if it's not in a war, wars that are already over. What exactly are you fighting? Is it a word problem? Do you need a tutor? Has anyone checked your work?

Does the power you feel from impact, from punching, from penetration, a pistol's kick, jet propulsion, does it know who gave it birth? Does it know it was feminine?

In the end, it will come down to The Math, to word problems we are still uncomfortable with, like *Intimacy*. Like *Courage*. *Softness* and *Actual Courage*. Are you beating your people because you don't know how to fix your dirt bike?

When I finally tried to re-remember, as far back as I could, I arrived at a stuffed animal, a gigantic green octopus. Mom said, *No, it was a frog, not an octopus.* Said it was so big I would fall asleep on it or wrap myself up in it.

But I don't remember that. The only thing I remember being wrapped up in was an airplane. Sealed myself into it. Left for a tour. Jet propulsion. A letter in an envelope.

BEFORE FEALTY

Why am I attracted to barbarians? To men who dream only of becoming the mountain? Never the river. *Why attracted to straight? To oak? To bass? To* Dude, watch me lift this small planet and eat the last of its living?

Answer: *The illusion of power. The audacity of owning. The assumed license. The attraction to being automatically right.* Which is to say: *The idea that the work is done.* The hard work. *Will be done for you. That you get to make the laws and not live by them.*

In a dream, a young tyrant boy, blonde like I had been, in blue eyes and jackhammers, streaks of irreconcilable anger, paced the ramparts, castle top, glaring down at me. And spit. And every time he spit, I would say, *But I love you.* And again he would spit. And every time, I'd say again, *But I love you.*

Boy, we got tired of not understanding which one of us was weakest. The moment I turned my back, he jumped down onto the trust of me, pushed my face through a puddle of mud. *If I can't breathe, I will die here. Finally. It hurts too much to not know how to stop the war.*

FEALTY

There must be some reason my body needs me to love Ramzan
Kadyrov, the President of Chechnya. Sings the blues in flashes of red
in the ring. Into a branding iron. You know the drill it through my
skull. Brother of Texas. Big man beats gay boys into the grave for not
cooperating with rocks. Thinks our power is weakness. Takers take
advantage. It's what they do.

Ramzan, my love, I too took a long time to understand how the
lightest things lift higher. Specific thread we pull. This is not a matter
of rope. To string me up by the throat bone. To put me in a stalker
chalk outline. I know you're just being a good boy. For Russia. For
Dad. Formal acknowledgment of your loyalty to the lord. The
great overcompensation.

Great apes, with a striking ability to imitate their fathers, who force-
fed those boys elbow grease alcohol, full of fist, and bash, wet sand
slung from a cup across concrete. Watch me wipe my mouth like it
was leaking blood. Goddamn. More and more the size of you. The
illusion of power. Filling up the day. With men. Not stopping.
From spreading.

Russia has the biggest land mass of any country in the world. It
has pulled you into itself. The frozen distance of virility dresses up
like a guarantee. Claims top spot. Controls the pleasure. Bravedick.
Off to war to play with the boys, in the image of bending steel.
Ramzan Kadyrov with a missile between his legs, in a cage match,
on the front page, on the front porch, with a smile in your mother's
arms. Do you cry to the boys when you're drunk then beat up the
cocksuckers to make up for it?

In an interview with Bryant Gumbel, you said that even if America
destroys you, the nukes will still go off. Said you would take us from
behind. The irony. The intuition. Ramzan, it may take ten thousand
years of no one reacting until you finally run from the roof, a light
thing lifting, but your body knows it's coming. Impermanence will
make light work of you,

Ramzan,

no matter how upright you pose in pictures, like the President of the
United States at Mar-a-Lago. Putin on horseback. All the boys inside
you: Boko Haram, before they found out their keys won't unlock the
schoolgirls they stole for a shot at purity, for a way to climb back
into the womb.

Women, there's a reason them boys are all mad at you. Giving birth
to the beast won't kill him. He will get back at you. The suffering.
What were you thinking, letting your pipes burst before the bubble
does? Everybody spot-mopping spit. The hocked-up history of it.
The last of its living.

Ramzan Kadyrov in a belly full of bruises, living a life
as large as Armageddon pie, wanting to die 7.5 billion times inside
himself instead of once at an easy pace, places an order for the drag
queens, dressed in guns and green. *Sweetheart*, she probably calls
you, your dumb mother. *Brother*, he probably calls you, your dumb
America. No better were the babies born before the day she bombed
us with you. No worse was the wait inside.

Years from now, the enlightened civilization ahead of us will stare
bewildered at our lethal masculinity and say, *But each one, when he was
running, tied bows to the top of his feet.*

Accidental Impersonations of Death

More often than not
encounters with snakes are harmless.
                    But sometimes…

            Eve—
who would later be named The Nighttime,
    who would go on to be known as Darkness
—said,
I'll be
  goddamn.

Farmly

Once, when we were way back when, we took our only family photo
at an Olan Mills inside of a Sears Roebuck. There were eleven of us.
We were shaped like breakfast. Biscuits mostly. American biscuits.
Don't call me a scrambled egg if you wanna keep your teeth.

That day, we were each allowed one bad choice from the bargain
rack, summer clothes that lasted a single wear before we stained
them green with grass in the knees, hands scraped from breaking
falls. Breaking falls because always falling. Being dirty was never in
question. Being poor was a rumor we believed in.

All the aunts. All the cousins. All those cheeks. No one's father
turned up and it turned out to be a pretty good picture for loud
people, who only talk that way to distract you from the stains they
are wearing. Worn out. I got it backwards and made a career directly
addressing the stains. I have enjoyed my job, mostly. Shit gets clean. I
mean, look how happy I am. Now,
get me out of this goddamn body.

When we tried to leave Sears Roebuck, Aunt Trudy was
stopped and questioned for shoplifting a pair of jeans.
That day, she didn't do it. All parties involved were very surprised.

It was the same day my cousin, Justin, slammed his finger in the car
door and broke it. He yelled so loud I dreamed about cough syrup.
He was unwilling to love us again until we could get him proper
help. We haven't seen Justin in years.

Before that, we were playing freeze tag around bossy drunk folk at a
family reunion where the unhealthiest among us were given the most
respect. I suspect, by that point, I had already surrendered to shock
treatment, the kind passed down from one unfortunate belief to
another. The thing about believing in what you were told to believe
in, is that you were told to believe it.

I was nine. Today I am forty-four, figuring out how to write this letter to a family of survivors and praise them. Cleanly. We are still growing out of these clothes we chose, every Sunday, dressed like faded blue Christmas trees in an attempt to oblige the unwritten dress code of rigid white Baptists who do not clap for the singer when the singer finishes feeling a hymn with her voice out loud. Lily-white whipped and fresh off a farm we never owned, until Aunt Tina and Uncle Bobby bought cows.

Once, when we were way back when, before Morgan was born, before Jess or David and Tommy, our sweet little 350-pound paranoid schizophrenic overlord, Memaw Verne, Lillian Laverne Montgomery, my grandmother, was at the Rusk State mental house subject to years of shock treatments, the kind passed down from mouth gags, made out of thick cotton batting and snake oil, to scrambled egg after scrambled egg after scrambled egg, back before that was widely accepted as a really bad idea.

Her holy Texas chainsaw. Her leather. Her heart.
Her love was afraid to tremble but it did, y'all.
She shook the room when she walked and spoke in great grief catastrophes. The government lived in her ceiling vents. *Crazy* is an easy word to say. *The Devil* is an easy name to speak. *Darkness* is a super artsy concept. I will enter through the mouth with a splintered flagpole and buttfuck your ancestors if you ever come near my cousins, Doctor.

On Sundays, Laverne would anchor the end of a pew, roll all seven grandchildren into a dust cloud and walk us from her house in Kilgore, Texas, for ten minutes, all the way over to the church next door. We were always late. We were always fever and light. Exhaustion was never in question.

Each week, she would unravel a roll of Life Savers then pass them down to spare each of us thirty seconds of Brother John's boredom. Suck a mint. Freshen our death. While she ate a banana and smacked it like there was good oatmeal stuck to the sides of her tongue, back when God was still a bad father, before the Lord finished clearing His throat of the dark ages, when I didn't know the color of my skin was such a murderer, before I realized how deeply my people hurt the earth, using words that rhymed with trigger, doing deeds that rhymed with bang.

Mother. Lover. Gospel. Fucker. Privilege is an unpayable debt. You owe me nothing. I didn't even see it coming. I never even saw it coming when my cousin Lace passed me the hymnal book, rolled her eyes back, trapped a laugh behind her breath, and pointed to the title of a song called "I'm Goin Home."

We laughed so hard, I got fat and ate drugs for twenty-five years, too terrified to wake up because what if the gay gets worse? Joy can be so insulting. It was everyone's equal fault. Damon, in case no one ever told you, you should have never been yelled at in the first place. You were an angel. So perfect, I put the word *angel* in my poem, and that shit is real uncomfortable for me, boy.

We do not need the South to understand us. We need the South to understand itself. Animals, except for the filthy ones, they only say what they need to. I am talking to tell you to stop. Family, fasten your breath to your bodies and watch.

If we accept these bodies this will all be over. It's never not been a good heart. Deliver us from the overworked language in our poor excuses. Having lived a shitty life does not mean you've *seen it all.* You've seen a ton of shittiness. Look alive, cousins. Prove nothing and call it grace.

Let's all spread out and search this place for the best ways out of Houston, without carrying each other's anger. Good God. When I try to remember what came before us, before this life, I sometimes get caught up in how nervous my family is to finally get to be with each other in *this* world.

Effective coping skills, they weren't affordable when we were kids, and nobody got any for their birthday. But we do have a picture of a people, trying, so hard. Smiling loudly. Shaped like breakfast. Scrambled eggs, mostly.

Once, when we were way back when, after Lynn picked his own switch, after Laney moved out, before Jay went into corrections,

Laverne left this world.

Rise and shine.

How can you still be standing there so blankly?

—**Library**, after throwing everything it had at them

LOSING DANNY OLIVER

Imagine, here, a montage of two lovers meeting, summer solstice,
a parade, eating in the park, walking to the sea, along the beach,
collecting driftwood, kissing at the window in a high-rise over the
city, buying a home, sex in the backyard, collecting the plums,
planting the garden, making dinner, eating with the neighbors, with
the house guests, at the local bar laughing, jogging through the trails,
adopting the dog, the two geese, the four ducks, and the chickens,
the tire swing, a note slipped between the warm folded laundry that
read, *I love you, Buddy W.* Then out loud he says, *I will love you
forever.* The joy. The pain. The end-of-summer party.
The death of Thanksgiving. The kill of Christmas.
Pulling for a breath while packing.

At the tail end of 2013, I left Steve. Stephen. Snook, my humble
barbarian, who I believed was the love of my life. Left our home, our
animals, our work together, and our daydreams. When people asked
why, I was full stop. It's hard to explain the gaping wound of distance
without a bridge to prove the span of its gap. I wasn't sharp enough,
when put on the spot, to label the dark side of serendipity with my
scribbly list of bad timing, lost reception, and
the suicidal tendencies of purpose.

My self-hate was fruit-fly-ripe. I'd been throwing it across the
kitchen, unable to control the danger in my feelings of isolation
from what I saw as his privilege: his comfort with body, his ease
with Earth. I wanted in on his ease with Earth, the salt of it; began
resenting Steve for holding back any empathetic relief when the going
was toughest. I couldn't gain access to his evident safety, the practical
way of being he seemed to enjoy. I was nosedive, an unreliable
narrator in an echo chamber. Speculation megaphone. Dying to
distill the anger and hear what was left.

My extensive inexperience in partnerships was a tar pit. To the rest of the world I was presenting an unrealistic Instagram image. Apple pie hot shit hot mess. I was offensively unhappy, my useless passive aggression a hood ornament. Maybe he knew how to love himself more than others. Maybe I loved others more than myself, for what I thought they were, instead of witnessing them clearly. I wish I'd known that witnessing this life clearly is the love we deserve.

Sick with flu-like symptoms for the fifth time in three months, physically and emotionally warped, chalking it up to stress, I walked out.

Thirty minutes later, I moved into an Airbnb, the basement of a house on Bainbridge Island, WA, to finish booking a sixteen-month, 230-date world tour called Riled Up and Wasted on Light (Skipping Chechnya). The tour would start in three weeks. The tour poster had already been chosen. Before all was said and done, I would very much look like the poster, but without the hat, the hair, or the chaps. I also never tuck my shirt in, but you get it.

BUDDY WAKEFIELD · RILED UP AND WASTED ON LIGHT

There was too much work for one man due to set off on tour in just three weeks. Other than a stint with a colleges-only agency from 2004–2010, and a little recent help in the U.K., I've been my own manager, booking agent, travel agent, merchandise coordinator, promoter, writer and performer, the whole way. I don't recommend it. If you're a former organizer reading this and thinking, *That's not true. I planned Buddy's event with a guy named Danny Oliver.* I was Danny Oliver. Danny gave me the ability to be hard-nosed in negotiations without sacrificing the artist you were hiring. I knew that if you Googled "Danny Oliver" you'd have to sort through thirty million results for a Michael Jackson impersonator. Danny Oliver was pretending he was not living in crippling grief. Now I just let people know it's me.

On 12/28/13

Facebook was ablaze that night over an article released about my friend, Ani DiFranco, planning to host a retreat at one of America's largest former slave plantations. "Righteous Retreat in the Big Easy" is what the organizers called it. I had agreed to participate in the weekend event and give writing workshops. What I didn't know was that I'd agreed to present workshops at one of the largest former slave plantations in America, a place still conducting tours that spoke of how well the slaves were treated because they got showers and Christmas gifts, for starters.

The promoters made the event look like an unconscious, white wet dream parading through a field of idiot flowers. One of the original articles released made it look like Ani and the participants knew the details of our destination. We did not. We knew about as much of the history of that venue as I do the house I'm sitting in right now on Serenbe Art Farm in Chattahoochee Hills, GA. Which is to say, nothing. The name Nottoway Plantation alone should have jumpstarted a quick research mission to learn the venue's history. But I didn't do any research, and I should have.

When I was asked over the phone to participate, I heard *Nottoway Plantation* and thought, *I've only ever heard that word in association with slavery, but it's 2013 so surely this is an agricultural reference.* When, in the same phone conversation, the agent told me Toshi Reagan, a powerful black artist from New York City, had also agreed to do the retreat, I paid no more mind.

Agitated by dozens of people assuming the worst on Facebook, many from the poetry community, I grew tired of reading post after post after post about what a piece of shit Ani was. And me. My eyes had a headache. That awful night.

I typed out a narrow, butt-hurt, knee-jerk response to the situation. It read like a defensive sixteen-year-old who had his cell phone taken away. I fell asleep without sending it. When I woke up, I couldn't help but first have a look at how the conversation had evolved overnight.

It felt like I'd stepped into a room, at capacity, of people swinging on my friend, teeing off from every angle. Occasionally, I'd catch a sucker punch, but nothing worth sabotaging my career for.

A white fella pretending to be the leader of the international shame fest posted, *Ani, you've got exactly three hours to explain yourself.* When it was followed by a posturing white woman, swimming in entitlement, and beating up my name, I clicked *Send* on that stupid post I'd drafted. That's when the universe said, *Oh, is it someone's privilege you're angry at? Well, watch this...*

Avalanche.

The hive. Hundreds of furious fuck *you*s. Every stinger on deck. In from every angle, often from folks I respected. I'd failed to address the most important thing buried under all my defenses, the root of the issue, my duty to use my own privilege to advocate for people of color, their well-being, and their dignity.

The post received far more attention than I expected. The call from CNN's *Raw Story* was a surprise. Having the post reprinted in local papers was a kick in the dick.

Over a decade of work and love with the poetry community, then in one knucklehead response, absolute failure.

Even after the initial reactionary mistake online, I made more. And more. And those mistakes became more and more revealing, not only of how much understanding I actually lacked, but of how dubious my fundamentals became when faced with *a lot* of people not liking me. There was considerable scrambling to save face while attempting to take ownership. Those two things are not compatible in an apology.

I was ashamed about attempting to control the damage instead of accepting it. Sickened by fast becoming an apologist, I had no more energy to do anything but take the beating. Members of the community I had loved for sixteen years, leaders who charge hearts on social justice issues, poets giving necessary voice to personal evaluation, keen quick-witted artists I champion, they were showing me their backs. Many of them I eventually lost to impatience and shortsightedness. Mine.

I sent an apology to a group of women in the poetry community. I couldn't bear them believing I was anything but an ally. I needed them to know I would get to work immediately installing mirrors in my blind spots. One of those women asked me what I learned. I told her I wasn't ready to answer. Despite her pressing me again to answer, I didn't. I'm only now ready to say:

I learned how to continuously watch which direction my thoughts sway on every matter of race, or where any oppressed community is in question. I learned that I didn't have a solid handle on the scope of systemic nuances in the matter of waking up. I was indeed out of touch, but, thankfully, only to a reconcilable degree.

I learned to comb through my defensiveness and take time with the snags. I've learned to not pretend my work around race is done, to ask questions, to relentlessly point a finger in the right direction, to move slow with what's fragile, like evolution does.

I learned that white people hate how hard I'm being on myself. I learned that apologizing any longer would make me a liar. Everyone, especially me, is sick of hearing me apologize. I've learned that I have to abandon shame and stick to the inner ring of my ripple effect. I'm learning my role in all this, that it doesn't require the same approach as yours, not if I'm to genuinely cause effective change among the people I'm responsible for, with whom I was raised, those who helped raise us, and those I am raising.

I've learned patience in talking to people who criticize the outrage of people of color instead of critically thinking about what's causing the outrage. I learned that the outrage is cellular. I learned about the abuses of power at every level, including the world of allies vying for position, that there are allies who pick and choose who and what to hold accountable, in the same way Republicans pick and choose their Bible verses, in the same way cops pick and choose who's going down for their transgressions.

I am learning new words to try and keep up with respecting others. I am learning how highly uncomfortable privilege is with bearing witness to anything outside itself.

I learned that humanity's inhumanity has a lot to do with needing to be right. I am still learning to release the need to be right. I learned that I was capable of carrying more than I thought was possible while still giving due diligence to the safety of others.

To the people who are ever dissatisfied, who cannot be pleased, I've learned your insatiable need for war at every level and in any name. I learned to not be intoxicated by anger. I learned that compassion does not expire. What I learned most came from reading these two things:

1.

This is one of those places where taking it in, the parts you agree with and the parts you don't, and just sitting in them, is essential to the dialogue. This is [a] place where you just listen. Not forever but certainly for now. The dialogue is happening all around you. You don't need to conduct it. Sitting and listening even when you have tons to say, even when you just wanna say 'see I am not the only one' is uncomfortable but is an act of solidarity. It is relinquishing just a bit of privilege. You know what you see. It is what you don't see, that is where the growth is.

—**Sonya Renee Taylor**, author of *The Body is Not an Apology*

2.

I had a boss who was racist. Not an outright bigot, of course; her toolbox was more subtle than most. We bumped heads a lot over inconsequential things. She frequently couldn't keep my name out her mouth. Lot of gaslighting. You know…2018 style. I tried a lot of ways to combat or navigate her issues. None of them worked, and that's saying a lot because I'm really good at fighting racism. But at the end of the day – every day – she was my boss, I had to deal with her, and that was that. Finally, I changed my job. I still had the same boss, but our work was far enough from direct contact that it was almost like not working together. I would still see her every day, but now I didn't have to contend with her behavior. I was free to do what I needed and wanted to do, and so was she.

I changed the power structure of our relationship because appealing to her humanity was a lost cause and I spent years learning that the hard way. It wasted a lot of time because I kept setting aside the truth: that racism is not about feelings; it is about power. Not being aware of that — making anti-racism work about friendships and tokens and tone — is part of why people get confused about what many black people want politically. We don't assume you don't know what racism looks like. And if it turns out you don't know what you're doing, we're often content to just get on with our lives because there are way more of you than there are of us, life is short, and our lives are statistically even shorter. Black folks literally ain't got time for that.

We're not out here trying to fix your racism. We're trying to make your racism have as little effect as possible. Anything else is misdirection, a mistake, or icing on real work already done.

—Scott Woods

Nothing is as blunt as an orchestra eating shit.

—**The Cymbals**, crashing

NOSEDIVE

Never

met

the

people

who

clean

up

the

crushed

parts

after

airplanes

crash

but

I

am

certain

that

when

w

e

pass

ea

ch

other

on

the

street

they

recognize

me.

TETRIS

I turned up late for a doctor's appointment right around the time they stopped taking patients. The receptionist, a mirror of my own heavy heart, was worn out, intentionally impolite, and encouraged me to reschedule then leave. A second receptionist appeared and whispered something to the grumpy one, then hurried off. The tone changed. I was seen by the doctor immediately.

I was waiting for the doctor in the room alone when he finally walked in.

Has the health department contacted you?

That was the first thing he said to me.

Any gay man whose ever been tested for an STI can tell you what that question means.

I have never felt so alone.

There is a brief, haunting moment in the otherwise comical movie *Ant-Man and the Wasp*, where a subatomic state is reached and everything goes deathly silent. That's where I was. Where the pain actually breeches its own expanse.

I left the doctor's office and sat in my car. Returned a text about the tour. Thought, *I can't believe you're texting right now.* Put down the phone. Walked into a grocery store, not at all hungry. Filled a plate at the salad bar. Walked it upstairs. Stared out across the rafters. Stared at a wall. For a long time. Put the grocery bag in front of my face, but it couldn't hide the sound.

I was so full of the feeling of failure that pulling the restart trigger began to work its way through every chamber in my thought revolver.

There's a video game called Tetris that drops blocks from the top of the screen. It's the player's job to fit each falling block with the blocks on the bottom, to eliminate completed rows of blocks. At higher levels the blocks fall faster and faster until it's nearly impossible to keep up with all the falling blocks. Then it's just game over. The screen fills and you're fucked. Years earlier, on my papaw's Game Boy, I beat Tetris. A rocket ship comes out at the end.

There were three things keeping me alive:

1) My father killed himself three months before I graduated college and the phrase "like father, like son" didn't sit well with me.
2) Meditation. It is my understanding that whatever suffering is left of me when I die will translate and travel with me. On days like today it's the only reason I stay here. When I go, I do not want to take this beast with me. Not one more step.
3) I beat Tetris.

THE CRUSHED PARTS

I was in the airport sobbing on a landmine.
A woman wearing a blurry face
that I could not wipe off
stopped to ask how she could help.
Nothing has ever hurt like not knowing the answer.
I told her I'd live.
And, so far, I didn't lie.

MISSOULA GOT UGLY
For 2014

Bridget the bartender at Brooks & Browns on the
flip side of the front entrance to the Holiday Hotel on
Pattee Street in Missoula, Montana, told me an old
Catholic saying once that went something like this:
You cannot let the sun set on being pissed.
    This was my failure.

There is a pattern I have worn
into my pillow with bad days.
There's a street lamp

so sick of shining on pavement,
an impatient plaster cast of kindness,
drizzled in the efforts of a greedy moth.

Don't just stand there with your hand on the kill switch
watching like a wasted wish.
Turn me off.

I have so much blood,
when I wake up
it rumbles under my ears,

a stampede of blazing horse rabies
barreling toward my threshold.
Put your head to my plunging chest

if you still don't believe
they are constantly coursing,
through my hiding spots.

They find me
breathing too loud.
I have been pulled out by the ankles.

I have been strung up by the brains.
In these bones,
it is my understanding

that whatever suffering is left of me when I die
will translate and travel with me.
On days like today

it's the only reason I stay here. When I go
I do not want to take this beast with me.
Not one more step.

I know better
than to call a thing good or bad.
I won't say that Hell is inappropriate.

These detachment lessons are brilliant
and burning.
Who can sleep like this?

These bursts of beast in my
blind reactions
belligerent and bombing around

the space between that
matte black pancake pavement gum
and the fat-lipped face of light.

I have been furious with this life
for being so blatantly beautiful
while I shake

the haunted shape of your vacancy
out of the window in our bed sheets
to release myself from wilting

in the way you walked away.

There is so much blood in me,
when I sleep
it pushes against my teeth.

Waterfalls pound the rocks to paste.
It tastes
like smoked salt and thimble slits,

like boorish work for the bed sweats.
How much hunger
do you think you can you feed a dying pig,

Earth?

You dirty mother's apron,
smeared in father attacks
and embroidered children

who laughed while walking backwards
watching me try to catch up,
watching me try to calm down,

trying to sew my lips shut,
double-stitched,
horsehair and bar breath,

startled by the grief in our common thread.
While I was eyeing the physics to needlepoint,
it began to make astonishing sense—

moths
too eager for streetlights
should not be in charge of sutures.

Look at this goddamn mess.
I constantly turn my pillow
to feel the cool side on my neck

so the tar in these lungs will level,
pave the way to safety,
unfold my forehead to the ceiling,

open letter
to the victims of my bad behavior,
dense venom

gone unchecked in my music.
I have been trying to stay composed.
The lyrics to candle spit.

Lately,
I am a lonely country
waving a landscape of flags

across the consequences
of intentional language:
fireflies in prison jars.

Bald tires on ice.
Guardrails
that will not go the distance.

Jungle gym bars.
These oily hands.
Missoula got ugly.

Mississippi kiss me.
A howling rush of simians
rising through the throat

of a white boy begging
to rearrange privilege
so he can return to fitting in again.

Safety is not my partner.
Comfort did not grow up here
in daylight under the bed.

All the anger I found in your maps to kindness,
in the groove where I was gutted,
a shovel shell of red lights in a tin can full of roads.

My blood moves through me so fast
it splits us like a tuning fork,
fighter jet threaded through a house fire,

rolled in the flicker of an aerosol can,
bursts of boiled foam in the mattress
where my head was supposed to rest.

There was no rest when you lived here.
Warm went the whistle from a cold metal man.

Sarah Healy, the ocean-swimming mother of
women with big feet, on the flip side of the front
entrance to the cathedral off Bassett Street
in Petaluma, California, told me an old personal
realization once that went something like this:

The lesson
will be repeated
until you learn it.

A STAY-OKAY BOX

Fifteen minutes later a doctor prescribed me lithium.
The root of the issue
always chews a hole through the drug.

To make light, you came home from a day of landscapes.
Demanded to see my wrists.
Pretended I was pitch black lipstick and bangs.
I laughed. Your bold moves.
The train that gave you singing lessons.
Reminded me you weren't against me. I needed that.

We answered to no one.
Except each other. And even then
we answered to no one.
By now I have no memory what the question was.

When I couldn't find my writing desk for two years,
you offered to leave. Only if it would break my heart.
I reminded you I don't get off on tragedy anymore.
And we both believed me until I could not stop crying.
I am so homesick, my love,
but not for anything on this Earth.

People who like their bodies
can't imagine a grief like this.

You said you wished we could trade places for a day,
so you could build in me a stay-okay box.

I put my arms around your head and held you
like a murder mystery I didn't want to end.

At a hotel in Portland,
we didn't have the cash to leave a tip,
so we stripped the bed sheets and gathered our towels.
Made an easier day for housekeeping.
Forgot what the distance between us felt like.
A sledgehammer 'round back. Heavy

like the day you didn't come home for Thanksgiving.
You wouldn't say you were sorry to save our lives.

When I woke up, your eyes darted sideways
and walked out of the room.
I could not follow along, tracing over an outline
of the way I wished I was you
                    No, I will not eat lithium.
when you were leaving here without me.

ENOUGH

There's a telescope
in my lower tooth

so when the sky drops my jaw
I can see the truth,

how nearly every star shot in the heart
will produce

enough light
when it knows that it has to.

Thank you, Lord, for all the ways you made us feel safe,
even if it was just drugs.

—**My Closet**, on behalf of everyone in it

THE END OF THE WORLD TOUR PARTY

What had begun on December 28, 2013, with leaving and eventually selling my home while on the road, had now turned into the end of April 2015. Heavy drugs had worked their way into me. About two hundred sex partners had too, thanks to my obsessive monitoring of hook-up apps, and Sweden.

To feel redeemed in any aspect of my life, I quit drinking towards the end of tour. My way of coping had become so warped that when a man in Asheville, North Carolina, offered me a beer from his fridge, days into our crystal meth binge, I told him I didn't drink. I stood there, jaw twisting off the side of my skull, and told him I didn't drink.

The only time I found myself present and approaching happiness is when I was on stage; pretty much your standard episode of VH1's *Behind the Music*. The downward spiral was excruciatingly unoriginal, but the pain was comprehensive. And the love I once had, the love I hadn't had a chance to make peace with leaving, was moving farther into the distance. And the greater the distance, the heavier the grief.

I was desperate for reprieve and driven to find understanding. I could no longer sanely navigate the devastation. The only thing that made any real sense, was knowing I'd be going to a Vipassana center immediately following tour, that dark unholy bitch.
Please. God. Meditation.

The day of registration at the Southwest Vipassana Meditation Center in Kaufman, TX, could not come fast enough. Sixteen months. 230 shows. Western U.S. to Canada to Australia to Africa to Europe to U.K. to Iceland, back to the Eastern U.S. The drive back across the south, up the West Coast, back to Seattle for a show that dropped out last minute and cost me thousands. I sold the van in Seattle and flew South for two last shows before staggering into the open arms of Austin, where my friend, Derrick C. Brown, owned a home in the country called Ranch Dressing. He was throwing The End of the World Tour Party for me.

Family and friends from every angle would all be there, in one place. I was terrified. An utterly open wound. My heart needed a hospital bed. Away from the agoraphobia. All that sweat in my blood. My devil blood. I wanted to die. What party and why? Where was my love? Did he really not come? Was he really gone? I started to drink again that night to get through the party without anyone seeing me. Got stoned. I was so out of my mind that I couldn't speak a lick of sense when the time came for me to get on the mic and acknowledge the guests. The embarrassment. Excruciating. My mom watching. Please, Vipassana. Three more days until Vipassana.

Two days before the Vipassana course, I got ripped on wine in Arlington, Texas, with my best friend from college, AJ, and told him:

When Eckhart Tolle was twenty-nine, he basically wanted to kill himself, experiencing almost unbearable suffering, said, I cannot live with myself any longer, *then, suddenly bliss. His ignorance left the building. He walked around London parks in a state of bliss for the next two years, then wrote a book called* The Power of Now, *which got translated into fifty languages. Oprah bought him his own TV station. For as much as someone who's suffering unbearably can, Eckhart got a free ride.*

AJ put his hand on my shoulder, *Buddy, you know you're not gonna get a free ride, right?*

TOUR: THE BALLAD OF GODDAMN

There was so much blood on the road
you could bottle up thirteen songs.
Knuckle knuckle there was so much blood.
You could bottle it up.
You could bottle it up.

And there was.

There was so much road on the rise.
There was so much rose horizon, so much rise and I was
blue and fire bleeding purple to gold
and that's when I blew by.
I was lighting it up.
I was driving it up.

I was a

wheel cocked. I was the weight of my foot.
I was a bullet spit into a landscape rip.
Road bent into the shape of a whip
and I was driving it up
'til I was stripped of it,

of all the

battle magnets in an animal clutch.
We had a feral map. It meant the most to us. We was a
blood rush on a slick horizon. We had all growed up
into a rabid bunch,
into a chemical trail and you could bottle it up.

We were lighting it up.
We were lighting it up.

And when the—

when the emotional violence, finally,
took its toll on me
a desolation of train songs, blindly,
wandered down thirteen streets.
And all the ghosts up in the beams,
a sun–drenched mob of memories
were swinging pound for pound with who I claim to be.

And I was eating it up.
You could bottle it up.

I just so badly wanted to hug you.

—**Horse**, upon trampling him

THE WORK

Vipassana is a Pāli word. It means *clear insight*.

I showed up to the Southwest Vipassana Meditation Center in Kaufman, TX, with no expectations other than to work. My highest excitement. From 4 a.m. to 9 p.m. Work. For ten days of silence with no distractions, working according to the technique taught. No rites, no rituals, no guru worship, no bullshit. No reading, no writing, no eye contact. No talking. Observing just breath and sensations without reacting.

Despite having been to Vipassana meditation centers for ten years, I'd never worked so diligently in my life, showing up to practice the technique at every opportunity. To breathe. While resting. While showering. While eating. While walking. While standing in the middle of a sidewalk in the scorching sun watching a wave of hurricane anger leave my body.

The urge to strategize a new future was strong. The only thing I knew about my life, post-personal-apocalypse, is that I was flying to my friend Andrea's house in Boulder on the final day of the course. Outside of Ani, Andrea was the only friend who called to check on my well-being as I was being properly exiled the week the Facebook backlash all went down. The idea was to get reestablished in meditation in Kaufman, then fly to Andrea's in Boulder, and live there as long as necessary to find some balance. To see a therapist for the first time consistently. Repeating history was an awful option. I was certain therapy would reveal the Relationship 101 material I missed growing up. In the closet until age twenty-three, no real partnership experience until my thirties, I was due for some understanding.

Understanding began in Kaufman, Texas, on Day 6.

Day 6

On May 7, 2015, in Kaufman, Texas, bliss showed up.

We were on the evening break. The new meditation students were having fruit and tea in the dining hall. I was sitting in a chair in my room looking out of the window with the wonder of what the hell I was gonna do with the rest of my life hanging over my head like a bag of shit and a box of fans. The recovery of every awareness I'm about to tell you, it happened at dreamspeed. What you need to know for it to make sense is this:

1) Lane Stroud introduced me to Vipassana meditation in 2005. I'd come off a long tour, began crying to Lane that I was sick of hearing myself talk, and Lane said, *Hey, I know about a quiet camp.* I didn't care what or where it was. It already resonated and I needed to go.

2) Oliver Klomp was the first person I spoke to upon coming off the ten days of silence at my first Vipassana course. Olli and I became friends for life. After a meditation years later, Olli spoke to me about following bliss, so I went home and began to write down the list of my bliss, which remained blank. *Bliss.* A bigger word than Yes. The sonic landscape of before-words. Of after-words. Booming unrealized idea. I experienced nothing of this bliss I was told to follow. What kept coming to mind when I tried to list the bliss were sex fantasies, which only served to fuel anxiety.

3) Lane approached me in 2008 in an elevated state, wide-eyed and ready for the world, letting me know she was going to do what she always wanted to do: direct films. She was going to follow her bliss and be a director.

4) For fourteen years I worked at an international academic/life skills camp with high school students where the question was asked at every camp, *What would you do if you knew you couldn't fail?* My answer was to be an actor and, sometimes, when I felt really bold to the truth, to be in Cirque Du Soleil.

5) In following her bliss, after directing a solid documentary on the WNBA, Lane moved to Los Angeles.

6) In high school, at my neighborhood video store, there was
a woman looking for a movie I've still never seen called
Let It Ride, with Richard Dreyfuss. I heard her ask an
employee for help finding it. The clerk was unable to locate
the movie. In an unannounced moment of unflinching
unwillingness to doubt anything anywhere, an animated foot
stepped down through the inside of my head, through my
throat, one long painless step, down through my chest, and
into the source of me, clearing all distrust on the way.
A white arrow shot up out of my midsection, through my
chest and throat and head, out over my shoulder and, with
no look, no hesitation, no resistance, no judgment, I turned
around, pointed to the bottom right corner of a shelf in the
back left corner of the store and said, *There it is.*

And there it was. *Let It Ride.*

What happened on Day 6 at the Vipassana center in Kaufman
cropped up out of the same fearless place. Weaving upwards through
me, three-child on a maypole, in and out and lifting up, these
glowing welcome reminders:

- *This practice has never let me down.*
- *Lane is the one who introduced me to this practice.*
- *This practice is where I met my lifelong friend, Oliver Klomp.*
- *Oliver Klomp told me to follow my bliss.*
- *Lane followed her bliss and moved to L.A. to be a director.*
- *If I could do anything and knew I wouldn't fail, I'd be an actor.*
- *I'm moving to Los Angeles.*

And with no warning, I entered into clarity. My body: struggle-free.
The excitement: breeching itself.

Bliss.

Bliss: A Chronicle of the Voice, in Order

Bliss!
Wait, Bud, are you bi-polar?
I don't think so… This is bliss! Like Eckhart!
You know it probably won't last two years like Eckhart's.
That's okay! You are so happy right now! Be happy, Bud!
Isn't wanting to be an actor kind of vain?
Hey, Bud, enjoy this! It is so much love and you have done so much work!

Exclamation points are my last choice, but are the only choice above. They are otherwise a little out of my comfort zone, like high fives.

Not sure how long I sat in that chair realizing the initial bliss, but it wasn't long. I quickly became curious what would happen if I moved. If it would go away, startle me back to the low-lying weight of this life, the unlikely feeling of bliss thwarted by a simple change in position.

I stood up.

It's still here!
You probably won't want to be an actor when you wake up tomorrow.
That's okay. Hey, you don't have to protect me from this feeling, Bud. I'm okay.

All my aim was on respecting presence. Every observation welcome. All sensations were an opportunity to see the mind-matter connection, stockpiles of defilements dissolving, looking each one in the face until it passed away like some incompetent junior high bully.

Then, a bubble of thought popped like a tapioca pearl inside my left shoulder, spread gradually down my left arm, into my left chest and all the way to the top of my left knee. *The left side is the heart attack side* is what I thought. It was the most unnerving pain I've ever felt. It came on like a baby's wail, slow to build but certain to deliver that godawful shriek. I had a similar pain twice in college that was never explained. I'd always assumed it was a pinched nerve. But this time it burned when I exhaled. Burned the way restlessness would if you threw it in a pan. It hurt. Hurt like not being able to lift my arms to fight back in a nightmare. Nevertheless, somehow, bliss.

THE HEART ATTACK SIDE

Saṅkhāra is a Pāli word. It means *that which has been put together.* Density forming. A body. Becoming more and more dense. Billions of saṅkhāra each moment. Compounding. Craving and aversion and craving and aversion. Lifetimes of it, compounding into a way of thinking, a body's way of being. Limitation. Craving and aversion. Craving and aversion. Saṅkhāra after saṅkhāra, becoming more and more dense. Unless there's awareness.

A saṅkhāra starved of ignorance will not grow.

At 9 p.m. I went back to my room to rest for the night. With every exhale came the burn. The burn, a world tour of my nervous system. Each nerve claiming to be my number one fan. I was so curious how the bliss was housing the pain. It was digesting it. It felt like my duty was to just keep watching, without reacting, so the saṅkhāras could disintegrate.

Exhaling accelerated the bawling of each nerve, long after the last of the breath left. It was cumulative, so the more I breathed, the more intensely the burn burned. I would observe the entirety of discomfort as long as I could, until the sensation became so intense I would curl fetal, often rolling out of bed and onto the floor.

Is this a heart attack?
I cannot believe how happy I am!

Twice during the night I got fully dressed.

You should probably tell someone you're having a heart attack, Bud.
Do heart attacks burn? I thought it was more about pressure.

And, so, I would take off my clothes and get back into bed to investigate the sensations and try to not react again. Start again. Start again. Start again. The screaming nerves caused such a thorough restlessness in the body that if I stayed present with it long enough, the feeling would spread down to the top of my left knee and jolt my quad into a wild shake that threatened my ankle with whiplash, the way I imagine one would behave if a metal rasp were pulled hard and slow across their teeth.

Thank you so much, Buddy, for experiencing this.
How are you so happy about this?
I don't know, my man, but I'll take it! And thank you!

The discomfort would last as long as the bliss, through the night, until about 6 a.m., when what was left of both the joy and pain slipped back into each other.

Fluid cogs. A perfect fit. The mechanics of a body's business as usual.

THE MOMENTUM STORY

No prophet

claims to be a prophet.

But the son of God

will tell you who his father is.

My father threw a glass with nails in it.

Before it hit the ground, he reached enlightenment.

A glass with nails in it

will hit the ground running

through the tread

of a luckless man driving

spare tirelessly out of reach

from his wife was having a baby.

His wife was having the last straw

was him missing the birth of their boy.

Camel back broke and no warning

she went it alone with a baby

whose father went mad in the meantime,

whose son learned hate trying to figure it out,

the war he was entered into

until revenge.

My father threw a glass with nails in it.

Before it hit the ground, he reached enlightenment.

A Choir of Honest Killers

They named me Kenneth Zane Beasley III.
At age five I was adopted by a truck driver.
Became Buddy Marshall Stevens.
Didn't much care for that. A number of reasons.
So I changed it to Buddy Wakefield. My name
is Buddy Wakefield. I am part saint, part fraud.
Being human

has been a largely humiliating experience.
I would say that it's been humbling,
but I suspect humble people
don't use that word. They humble up,
Buttercup. We got ourselves some friendly names,
don't we? Got ourselves in a pickle, friends.
There are

no stunt doubles performing the devastation
in losing everything. Maybe
we are losing everything
on purpose. There's a good chance
I'm a bad person, trying to do something right.
It turns out

everyone is right. It turns out
we are happening
so fast. The whole world. So fast. Yesterday,
I was twenty-three. The day before that,
I was nine. And none of the soured relationships
were worth my need to be right.
Happiness

is too far to fall. And you, my love,
you were a skyscraper tabernacle, mouth full of water.
Beautiful and too far to fall. Oh
but look at us take a tumblequake. Yeah
look at us take our lumps. Look
everybody's headed for the pass again to
cut each other off.
If

my whole body and if
your whole body—if
every single one of our bodies—
got amputated right now,
we would still have to deal with what's left of us.
Everything we ever ordered. Now

The Waiter

who is very famous for telling stories
to make people feel
like they feel better than they actually do,
he strutted up to our table, a cocky lion
walking straight into the mouth of a whale, and said,
Put it in God's hands.

I said, *Boy, we* are *God's hands.*
Stop standing like an apology you never meant to give.
Your context is unruly. The waiter
reached across my audacity,
evenly placed the silverware, then politely replied,
Sir, you don't know me.
You know a mistake I made.
Now,

who ordered the worst-case scenario?
Maybe I did. Maybe you. Maybe on purpose
until everyone in the whole world
found out everything we were ever terrified
of being found out about, and no one
was impressed with our nightmare. Air

does not have an ego. Pay attention then
when it enters and exits. Each one of us
feels desire inside them and can point to it on a map.
Stop acting

like you don't know which direction your life
is going. It is hysterical
pretending to be something you're not. The loneliness
is so goddamn blunt. Everything
here on the ground is a trigger.
Don't expect to be warned again.
You're a

full-grown jawbone. Though I have zero proof
that any of us are adults. But
there is still a voice inside me
that believes we will make miracles
of the laughter left between us.
Recently,

I discovered a word
that will fix everything I broke in our home,
rescued it from my body, and passed it on
to people who will use it properly. You
finally leaned over to my ear,
whispered

so close to my throat
it fogged up the knife, spoke
what you thought was my name until
I could not remember where I came from,
then patiently waited for me to explain
what in God's crippled name I am even
talking about.

So I clenched your history. And
I pulled it out of repeat. And
I loved you forever,
while we all sang these words
like a choir of honest killers
learning to leave the beast behind,

If I go forth from this world without you,
I did not forget to survive
the both of us.

I would never hurt you, but I might forget the things I do
and the things I say that might.

—**Grief**, to everything attached

Two Things

It was the last day of the meditation course. I walked my bags to the dining hall to wait for my ride to the airport, which is when Matthew walked up, smiling.

Matthew was the center manager for the Northwest Vipassana Center south of Seattle, where I had gone for most of my sits since beginning the practice in 2005. During volunteer service periods, Matthew and I had become friends and I knew him to be a thoughtful, kind, curious man. You can imagine my excitement, realizing I'd get to spend the last twenty minutes in Kaufman, TX, on a walk with my old friend from the Northwest.

We dove in straightaway and I told him about the bliss, and the pain in the left side of my body. I told him everything I could. When I was finished, he said, *The left side of your body is the feminine side.*

We dove into Matthew's world, his marriage, his involvement at the center and his practice. We strolled back to my luggage right on time and, before we parted, best foot forward, he said to me this:

I feel like I'm supposed to tell you two things: One, you don't have to help anybody right now and, two, it's okay to make a mess.

The next week I had my first therapy session with a man named Bruce Tift in Boulder, Colorado, a thousand miles away. Will you believe me when I tell you that at the end of our session, Bruce tacked on a final statement as I left, a non sequitur even, saying,

I feel like you should know two things: You don't have to help anybody right now. And it's okay to make a mess.

Rumble and Comatcha

Some breaths come
like a stomach pump
backed up
moving through an abscessed
front tooth
spoke
a message
in a bottle of rocks.

Some breaths
happen like a face plant,
blood
on an ink blot,
fluent
as a belly flop, square
knot rope
from a steel cut umbilical vox.

                              You knew you
              couldn't play the vocal cords properly, Pink,
         so you hadda try your luck on the fuse box parts.
              Sparky, I don't mean to say
              that the tunnel through your borders here
                    ain't worth a midnight ride,
                 but the wallowin you're doin
                       is entirely ineffective,
           like a waterfall fight with fireworks moving
                          in two totally
                       different directions.

Oh and I came down with force,
cold bag of rice on a bed of forks,
while it was lookin like you were the law.
Ain't anybody here ever looked that hard.

Yeah and you were just doin your best.
Best.

Some breaths come like a pillar of salt.
Some leave like a high-rise down,
core the wind like an apple
crab
trap kill an elephant
tree
trick tourniquet
twisted up into its benevolent trunk.

Some. Some breaths bring about
a lie to the room
for the rest of us to swallow whole,
Zen koan defibrillator
current
cardiac arrested
blind
carbon copping fields of that poisonous junk.

Oh but I couldn't keep that pace,
bug on a road in a high-speed chase,
while you pretended to be the law, like
nature's gonna break its rules for the wrong.

Yeah and I was just doing my best.
Don't mention it.

Pink, you know I was the favorite cake
you took and ate too,
called it righteous, left the fork in my neck,
knowing good and well I never meant
you didn't win the bragging rights
to misery and
sex with impending doom.
It's just the damage that you're doin
is entirely fuck-infested,
molasses-soaked and razor-backed
revenge on the men
in your blood orange moon.

Some. Some breaths go
like a mother
in a green light
driving
to a stop sign.
Some of them are taken away
by your leather daddy
tattoo
whistling
a land mine,
a note for every standard
doubled
down on the way
to every lover you were looking for a reason to slay.

Overwhelmeth

When the pressure in the bridge of my nose pulls to
anger, and my head contests the rails in my neck,
when the shortness of my breath turns to red,
and I'm a riot from the fever digging out of my chest,

I tend to bury underneath a pile of fenders bent.
I tend to shout about the lock in my jaw.
I tend to look for air to turn to forms of flying again
until I rescue up the habits of G—ah ah.

If there were nothing blind about my reactions here,
if the patterns I have carved in the land,
weren't subject to the laws of the thick of it,
weren't gathered in the sleight of my hand,

I would double up this penchant for sitting still.
I would put the pressure proper to ease.
I would lead the rest of what I keep shutting out
through the tunnels turning toward our release.

Race me through the pockets of air streams strummin,
running circles 'round the ringers of dystrophy.
I'm gonna ride a banner out of my chest unchained
'til you can read it arching out of the spray.

There was no one ever under my bed that day
waiting for the night to arrive, to terrorize the sheep I
count and kill to fall asleep, when they go leaping
like a stupid faggot into the light—my my my.

Yes, it was the worst of the best I could do
when I reacted to the way that a worm works a bird,
turning over leaves for the newborn things,
a little rusty with my window of words,

connecting dots between the party to the part that isn't
sorry, 'cause there's a part that isn't sorry inside,
when I see me going under, under agony and all.
I wonder how it is I ever survived.

There was a banner blowing out of my chest
on an arrow over oceans of stacked flat glass,
waves of understatements in resounding flash that read
Kill me and *Thank you* and *Goddamn, that's enough.*

And I don't know if the light was white, or flat, or even there. Can't say if my body was gone or just propped up in the air somewhere.

—Distance, coming for me

THE TWO OF CLUBS

When I see the number seventy-two, or a Ladder-backed
Woodpecker, or Pileated woodpeckers, or the two of clubs in a magic
trick, it is clear that I am exactly where I'm supposed to be. I do
not know how I know this. I just do, like a rooster knows to throw
himself between a coyote and the coop. Things that resonate often
lack the ability to argue. That's why I'm in love with you.

When I was seven, the dream was to be an adult
so I would have enough money to buy as many Pop-
Tarts as I wanted and there would be no one to stop me.
Why weren't adults already doing this? More proof
that I have always been a little advanced in my thinking.
Tonight, I am in my forties, having an egg
and a salad and soup. How did I get so dumb?

I'm a professional at getting out of the way,
at getting out of bed anyway, at getting my shit together,
at being this age and still working it out. My whole life
I practiced filling out job applications to myself. Poems.
It took years to get an interview. I don't remember the
date I started, but I would quit right now if it meant that
all I had to do was chop firewood in exchange for perfect
poems for the rest of my life. If I got one word per axe
swing, then at somewhere around every three– to eight–
hundred swings, I would have a perfect poem.

Every evening, I report my own nightly news.
In yesterday's live telecast there was a relay race to the
light, an emotional prison was de-privatized, and history
got revised to make it look like I chose the betterment of
humanity over sleeping in too often. In other news, we
lost my stepfather to a deer hunting instructional video marathon.

When water is running in any house that's not mine,
I can hear the voice of the youngest person who lives
there. We have to be able to talk about the truth in its
entirety. I get so lonely for the people I lost to not telling
the truth, to how weird it was in the curtains. Just
standing there in the curtains.

When I see someone to whom I'm incredibly attracted,
I silently say the word *Yes*. That means I get to have sex
with them in the afterlife for various lengths of time,
which I specified the moment I said *Yes* to them in my
head. Some for ten minutes. Some for two years.
I started doing this in the seventh grade.
When I die—if it worked, and if my calculations are
correct—7.2% of the world's population and I will hang
a *Do Not Disturb* sign on the appropriate realm. We will
see you again after approximately 720 lifetimes.
Sometimes I look forward to it. The only thing I worry
about is the boy I said Yes to forever.

Today, I wondered what would happen if all the water
immediately disappeared from the ocean, an instant
glimpse of what everything in it is up to: a hammerhead
attack on the octopus ink, synchronized shiners in an up
swirl, dolphin sex, the sails, before gravity. A jellyfish
crashing ballet. I want to see the ocean's action without
water in the way. Just once. If water were to get in the
way, the sun would take three minutes longer to reach
the Earth. Everything evaporates. Except whale sonar.
That's what I'm using to find you again.

My favorite pastime alone is to consider the connections
between two seemingly unrelated nouns. Marmalade and
welder gear. Satellites and Beans. Me and you.
Some days, I just don't see the relationship working.
Some days, I'm a verb. Those are the days I go missing
again. A polar bear in a snowstorm. A black cat at night.
I haven't seen my own reflection since the day you left
my life.

Sometimes, when I see someone I think I'd rather be
than me, I remember how we are really all just one
and that I'm actually the person I'm jealous of.
And whatever it is they're doing, I'm doing that.
And I try to adjust my location frequency to exactly their
action now. I am in the spot of my action.

So that no one in the rich neighborhood would question
me, a stranger petting their horses, I engaged the
kickstand on my borrowed bike. People who use a
kickstand are entirely non-threatening. I tip over more than I should.

At my last home, karma did not stop to say it was sorry
for the death of the woodpeckers when the ocean went
away. But it did hear a voice recite the chopping of wood
over the breaking of the nightly news, three minutes
slower than usual, seventy-two days' worth of Pop-Tarts
crammed into its lonely sex, watching me find the card it
hid up my sleeve.

SĪLA

Sīla, another Pāli word, is intentional ethical behavior according to one's commitment to the path of liberation. It is a moral compass within self and relationships, a commitment to what is wholesome. Honoring the precepts of sīla creates an atmosphere of security, trust, and respect. The practitioner poses no threat to another person's well-being.

What strong sīla looks like for me, and is expected of a student while at a Vipassana center, is an adherence to five simple tenets:

1) No killing.
2) No lying.
3) No stealing.
4) No intoxicants.
5) No sexual misconduct.

Well, what qualifies as sexual misconduct? asks nearly every supposedly progressive person who ever hears this tenet, and in a vibe akin to white fragility. The answer is for you to be honest with yourself about it. If it causes harm to you or others on any level, distracts from your practice, generates anxiety, or keeps you blindly reacting, then maybe give complete celibacy a try for a period. Experience celibacy before being appalled by it. Understand its purpose. It is not necessary to be upset with people who do—and experientially understand the benefits of—such work. It doesn't mean they're sex-negative.

Once I established a diligent foothold in sīla, my presence grew clear. My clarity was crisp. My human was tight. I was not about to turn back to a life of misery. Yes, balance is key, and not everyone finds it necessary, or feels capable of, living to the degree of self-restraint that I often do to locate balance. But, sometimes, I like to hit all the reset buttons, reset all the pumps, observe all the default settings, push all the runners back to the starting line, and set the scene for setting the table anew. So I did. I registered to attend another Vipassana course near Fresno, CA, six weeks later. Mid-June. Celibate.

MILKWEED

We were now in June. I hadn't jerked off since April 23rd. Hadn't ignored any of the other precepts either. My insides were glowing through to my outsides. Beaming. Following the day was becoming easier and easier. I bought an inner tube and floated down Boulder Creek as often as possible. Miles of it. Sometimes I got out for surprises, like the kids who'd soaped up a tarp on the side of a hill and were sliding down and running up and sliding down. I pulled myself from the creek when I saw them. One of the older boys noticed and waved me over. I was so excited. I ran all the way over to the cheering kids, and I ran up the hill, and the boy who waved me over went sliding, and I ran and I dove and I followed him, and we slid all the way down and across the wet grass. It was my forty-first birthday, June 4, 2015. I made this post to Facebook:

For weeks I've been listening to all things Eckhart Tolle on YouTube as I hole up in a sunny patch of Boulder, well-recovering from tour, having reluctantly sold off everything I owned once more, in order to detach, start over, largely living in a state of we'll see. Thank goodness. What's left is packed in a bright blue bag at the foot of a bed in the guest room of a friend's home. I just now found this clip of Jim Carrey introducing Eckhart Tolle, which happens to have taken place six years ago today (June 4, 2009, my birthday). I remember that day well. I'd realized a lifelong personal health goal. I could hardly be more on board with the volition in this video and what it represents. This post I'm posting is from a place of being stoked on serendipity, not a ploy for birthday wishes. Not necessary. This year, what I want is to introduce you to my love. Please, be a respectful family about the video clip I'm bringing home for you to meet. If you disapprove, maybe that's A-okay and you'll still find it in ya to bite your lip, watch it without comment, and just be happy that I've fallen in love again, with the point of this video. I'm probably gonna ask it to marry me.

The video was "Jim Carrey's Full Introduction for Eckhart Tolle" on Vimeo. And the point for me was serendipity. Somewhere within the introduction Jim says, *Let's have the intention of walking out of this place, or being blown out of here like milkweeds, and planting seeds everywhere we go, just putting a little bit of our intention in the things we do.*

The joy of that day was immeasurable. I'd see that a friend or family member was watching the video, so I'd watch Jim Carrey's whole intro again, through their lens, to guess which parts moved them most, or to wonder if they understood the moment Jim called to the woman in the very last seat, in the back corner of the room, and asked if she was aware that she created what we were all witnessing. Sure, it would have been great to hear from Steve, but I knew better than to expect it. I was just pleased to finally be in a space where I didn't consider him a necessity to happiness.

At 11:58 p.m. that night, I got a text from Steve and my heart pounded with thanks. It would be the perfect end to a bright day. He *remembered*, is what I thought. But the message contained no text, just a link to a video of the lyrics to a song called "Red Eyes" by The War on Drugs. The lyrics were vague, but what I read were the words to tell me he was moving on, that I had beat him down against his will, and that anyone could tell that the way I saw things was a lie; that I abused his faith and that he would be the one who finally couldn't take anymore. I lost track of myself and responded with the Hell inside, a long letter, composed of fragmented me. And insult. I was also secretly super pissed that he called dibs on such an awesome song to tell me those awful things.

When I saw him the following year, he explained how he was just sending me a song he liked.

Today is. Then today felt like it needed to make
that sentence longer.

—**Yesterday**, catching up, pissed

AN ACTOR

My mind was made up. The next day I told Andrea,
I'm moving to Los Angeles to be an actor.

Bud, I think it's perfect.

I called my friend Lane, the one who led me to Vipassana, who moved to L.A. to be a director. Lane said I might want to be in Los Feliz. I want to be in Los Feliz. I want to be there by October. I don't want to pay more than one thousand dollars a month. And it has to be furnished because I just sold or gave away everything I owned.

Bud, it's perfect.

Can I stay with you until October?

As long as you need to.

THE ACTOR

In the seventh grade
Jimmy Morin shoved me up against a brick wall,
held his arm across my throat,
and told me that if I didn't give him fifty cents a day
for the rest of the school year
he would beat me up.

I got a boner.

At least once a week
I would miss payment on purpose,
but Jimmy
never beat me up. His integrity
and business sense as a bully
were very bad.

Let me back up.

When I was four years old,
Lonnie Watson restrained me
in a game of cops and robbers. It was then
that I knew I was home.
When Lonnie's little brother, Calvin,
tried to pull Lonnie off me,
I kicked Calvin in his goddamn freckled leg.

I locked Lonnie's arms

so tightly across my chest
that Lonnie could not break free from
holding me captive.
I'm supposed to be the one making you my *prisoner*,
Lonnie said. *I know*, I whispered back. *Thank you.*

There has never been a time when I didn't know
exactly what makes my body move the blood around.

In first grade
Todd Hayes would wrestle me every day at recess, praise
the lord. Todd went undefeated
because of my favorite rule
of any rule in the history of sports,
the one that says you win
by pinning your opponent to the ground
for three seconds

of heaven.

Todd would tangle into my arms,
collapse his bruiser body over mine,
and hold me down as long as he could,
but I was a strong boy,
and I would lift my shoulder, two seconds
into every single one of Todd's attempts at counting me
out.

Don't count me out.

Acting is easy
when you know what your character wants.
It is not in my character to want a man to lose,
so every time Todd grew too frustrated
I would give in and let him pin me for the full three
seconds, insisting that I didn't know if I would ever be
strong enough to win.

But I do know

there are people who will think this is too perverted
because we were just children,
but they would be wrong,
because we *were* just children, roughhousing,
still learning how our bodies react to this life,

and I got beat up,

and Mom yelled at me because of the grass stains,
and I itched for days from the lawn clippings,
and Todd's shirt smelled like milk,
and that's as dirty as my thoughts ever got.
But my body, my body felt safe, and warm, and in
control of exactly how much of a beating
I was willing to take this life.

Let's take it to the tenth grade.

In the tenth grade never mind I can't tell you
about high school because they remember me there
and those dudes
eat a symbolic amount of steak. But I *will*
tell you about college because *fuckin college, amirite?*

I went to a university

that was number one in the country for criminal justice,
and number two, within itself, for agriculture.
What that tells us
is how the whole campus
was largely populated by cops and cowboys.
To you, that may mean nothing. To me,
it means a lot of time alone with a hand towel.

The first time I had sex with a man

I was nineteen. He was twice my age.
We met while passing each other on the stairs
at an afterhours club in Houston.
He asked if I wanted to do some crank and fuck him.
The music was loud so I yelled back into his ear,
I've never done that before!
And he yelled back into mine, *You snort it!*
And I yelled back into his, *That sounds unreasonable!*

When I was twenty-three

I finally stopped lying to people about being gay,
but I spoke nothing of the humiliation.
It's hard to tell anyone I dreamed of becoming
a housewife, when being gay is already so goddamn gay,
when I've already learned how to present as straight,
and, besides, it would be entirely unfair
to all the other women, how pretty I would be.

The only thing

that has ever made me feel comfortable
about being gay
was the crank. It turns out
crank is crystal methamphetamine
and crystal meth is the star of every movie ever made
about zombies, or the apocalypse.

Or both.

For twenty years, annually,
monthly if the valley was flooded,
the zombie apocalypse came knocking at my door
collecting psychotic tax breaks from my
short-term memory to remind me
of the only way I might ever feel worthy
without having to work for it.

So at age forty-four,

after three years of living in Los Angeles—
where I moved to continue my writing career
and become the actor I've already proven to be—
the hot zombie man on Scruff came calling,
told me it was time to pay up again
because I may never recover from the panic attack

of giving a shit.

Him tempting me into another week of life
in crystal bliss, holding out an oil pipe,
lighting a torch underneath it
and asking what it is I would most like to do
to feel good about my life, right now,
demanding that I answer him

quickly—

I sucked every life I've ever lived
into these dungeon lungs,
shoved The Apocalypse up against a brick wall,
threw my arm around his neck,
shot a cloud of smoke down the back of his throat,
and told him, in no uncertain terms,

I want you to make me play a role in a movie
where I get to act so gay
I can finally relax.

Mama's Boy

Is someone gonna tell me when enough is enough?
You better hold me down

if you want it to stop.

My dead daddy's makin his way to me now.
My daddy dead dead daddy daddy takin me down.

Wrappin around me, the wound unwound.
The how now now.

Now
is someone gonna tell me enough?

Don't walk away from me when I'm talking to you.

—**The Ocean**, to Land

AGES 0.1 TO 40 – SHREVEPORT, BINGHAMTON, NORTH TONAWANDA, SANBORN, BAYTOWN, FOSTER CITY, SOUTH HOUSTON, HUNTSVILLE, LA PORTE, PEARLAND, ARLINGTON, SEATTLE, HONDA CIVIC, ROTTERDAM, KINGSTON

There're so many creatures already crawling around this planet that I can't even begin to identify. Millions. Why would I concern myself with aliens? It's not that I don't believe in them, I just don't give a shit. Haven't seen one and probably won't. Not gonna go look for one either. There's too much other stuff happening here that I'm still trying to make sense of. I'm happy to consider us the center of the universe, what with this being the only life I know.

If aliens do come down, I'll behave the same way I would for Jesus, like, *Oh shit, my bad, Bossman.* I'd gladly concede, offer Him a hug, a hand with his bags, a hearty meal. But that's not happened. And it's probably not going to. I'm interested in eradicating suffering on this planet, not displacing my attention on other worlds looking for other life forms to add to the fray.

Age 41 – Boulder, Co

A friend came to town shortly after I moved in with Andrea. A lot of friends came to town. Life was a river of *absolutely* and I was over the moon about it.

Here's the thing about calling someone *best friend*: I don't feel comfortable doing it anymore. 100% is 100%. I'm fortunate enough to need two hands to count the number of people with whom I get to share friendship 100%. There is a lot of love for me in this world, and I can't imagine a sweeter thing to have been gifted.

One of those 100-percenters came to town not long after I arrived in Boulder, someone I trust as much as my mother. In the way that, if my mother sat me down and said, *Buddy, I have to tell you something you may find very difficult to believe*, no matter what it was, I'd have no choice but to consider it. I mean, it's my mother.

It's with that same earnest attention I sat with my friend and listened to what he had to say. We'll call him Dylan. It's hard to imagine a time in this life when Dylan and I weren't 100%. Dylan, with whom my safety and happiness are never in question. A friendship so reliable I consider it a personal responsibility to not invent the bullets I'd take just to show Dylan I would take a bullet for him. Haven't had to. Until now, maybe.

It started when I joked off on a comment about aliens. After some pause, Dylan said, *Buddy, we gotta have a talk*. Sometimes when Dylan looks at me all I can see is Sam Sheepdog from the Wile E. Coyote cartoons. Sometimes when I talk to Dylan, I put a pillow over my stomach and enjoy not feeling ashamed that I'm putting a pillow over my stomach because I often feel ashamed. Neither of us are entirely comfortable being human.

Buddy, if our friendship is going to progress, I need you to know why I'm really in therapy. I mean, the things you know already are reason enough, but... Listen, here it is: When I was a kid, an alien spaceship landed in my backyard. My parents saw it. My parents. Simple, basic, no frills people; they'd never make up such a thing. It would cost too much. The next night they went out and left me with a babysitter. Our neighbor ran over from across the street and asked the babysitter if she saw the spaceship that was just in our yard. What I can tell you is that they took me, more than once, and it wasn't through a door or a window.

Floored. I immediately thought of the movie *Communion*, based on a true story, how the entities must have breached the security alarm by moving directly to a location frequency. I thought about how scientists split an atom, put the two halves fourteen miles apart, charged one half, and the other half started spinning. Thought how now is all that ever was or will be. Every technology. Every capability. Thought about Eckhart Tolle. Vipassana meditation. How experiential presence kept exposing me to greater awareness of life just outside the narrow general narrative, showing me planes similar to those through which I traveled in supposed hallucinations as a teenager. Genius consciousness. Remarkable daylight. Anything's possible. Everyone's right.

The whole universe held my chin with the tips of its padded fingers, slightly turned my head a few degrees in a new direction, and my eyes opened into free fall. The aliens, in looking back, didn't arrive in my line of sight as a surprise as much as they did an excitement. Dylan had never seen anyone react to the news by getting so excited. The new information only seemed to strengthen the frequent specific serendipity ramping up its governance of my life.

The good fortune of precise coincidences has often appeared on my path. But it wasn't until after my tour manager, Kaylen, played piano in Georgia under the statue of the girl hugging a horse; wasn't until after I met the same hitchhiker a second time, a year later and a thousand miles away; when people, unprompted, began volunteering stories of their abductions. Wasn't until then that the serendipity became such a constant that I accepted it as verifiable.

Some moments are in alignment to such a degree that they might be mistaken for miracles. Serendipity is not miracles. Miracles aren't even miracles, just constant recurring reminders of how much we have not been paying attention. Available to every moment. Miracles are the normal in every moment.

Questions. I started asking Dylan questions. The answers arrived in a wad of anxiety, a constant shifting hesitation soaked in the potential for panic. Dylan did not possess my excitement. In fact, after resisting my attempts to exchange in speculation of how aliens were able to abduct him without the use of doors or windows, twenty minutes into the discussion, Dylan was overthrown in a flood of tears. I sensed his dying will to pretend the subject matter didn't cause in him a wholly terrifying trauma response, and he asked that we not talk about it anymore, for the time being.

I wanted to know everything. But I've been called out on enough blind spots to recognize when it's time to not say one more goddamn thing, especially to a devastated person still suffering an attack. Dylan looked awash in the helplessness of feeling like prey, of feeling like not the author of this story, sweeping gross sensations, a relic in a new science. I could tell, even under the effects of the poor health Dylan had been dealing with for months, one continuous unrelenting headache, even under that, talking about the aliens hurt him, even though it wasn't supposed to.

HORCHATA

Whatchew know about horchata? I asked him.

Man, are you serious? Did you know the word horchata *is in two of my email handles?*

I didn't.

What I know about horchata? Man, I fucking love horchata. Why?

Well, we're here an hour early, I said, *and I don't want to go in yet. There was a Mexican food place a couple miles back. Wanna get some horchata and keep this conversation going?*

There are over two hundred Vipassana centers around the world. After I left the one in Kaufman, TX, then arrived at Andrea's house in Boulder, I scheduled another sit at a different center, this one in North Fork, CA, near Fresno. The world tour savings would still have to last a year or two, so, to pay for the flight there, I booked a show in Fresno. Bryan, who fucking *loves* horchata, organized it.

When we booked it, Bryan offered to let me stay with him and his partner. There was a horse in their backyard the next morning with a veil on. I offered it a carrot. It didn't want the carrot, but it didn't mind me.

That day, Bryan drove me to the North Fork Vipassana center, an hour from his place. It was mid-June 2015, a couple weeks after Dylan told me about the aliens, who deserve less stigmatized names by now, I suppose. Ancestors? Polyticks? Research scientists?

I was still steadfast in my sīla, the tenets of a moral compass, and could hardly wait to reenter serious daily meditation at length.

We arrived at the Mexican restaurant still excitedly talking about Eckhart Tolle's *The Power of Now*, as we had been the whole way from Fresno. As I drank horchata, Bryan set down his burrito and said to me, *Buddy, I never get to talk to anybody like this. You speak my language. Can I tell you about my abduction?* The first forty years of my brain tensed up. But after weeks of precise arrivals, I knew to listen close.

Absolutely. Humans or aliens?

Oh, aliens.

Eight times that he could remember. They took Bryan eight times. I took minimal notes, with his permission. Here's exactly what I managed to type into my phone:

June 12, 2015
Regarding aliens: More than leather.
He sees [their eyes] as bees or preying mantis.
Orb. Pulsing. (Black dot then white).
About 8 times, with the last time being about 8 yrs ago.

Now, you can't be a forty-nine-year-old black man in this country and not have lived through some traumatic shit. I don't know that you can be a forty-nine-year-old black man *anywhere* and not have lived through some deeply traumatic shit. So, twenty minutes into my eager line of questions, same as with Dylan, when Bryan burst into tears, a distressed map of rivers rolling out from a lifetime of apparent helplessness to their choices over his body, I knew to stand down and let the new reality settle in. Bryan's story was different from Dylan's, but the details were the same.

As soon as I checked into the Vipassana center at North Fork, before I powered down my phone, I texted Dylan what had just happened, hit send, and pulsed in the presence of no going back.

Thanks, everybody, for repopulating Earth. I think we're all set.

—**Earth**, speaking in third person,
passive aggressively

NEXT LIFE SOUNDTRACK

Having pushed panic buttons / and pedal metal / down the throats of freeways / and crashed / like heavy glass ashtrays / into our own homes / broadside / with department store force and a gas can / distended stomachs / and all of God's holes—

Having shown off our momentum for yawning / as a clever way / to denigrate deeds of kindness—

Having created / enough minimum wage faith / to distract orphans from the exit rows / then thrown holding pattern parties / in their honor /only to present each other / with our own names /on gold plaques / bolted to a fountain of tollbooths used / to get dressed up up in our go go go and gone uninterrupted by the signs that serve to encourage calming down—

It is good to know / I have finally been loosening my grip / on the expectation / that our thumbs / will necessarily oppose each other / in the next life. There is a next life / and it is my understanding / we will not necessarily be binge-drinking bros / wearing Greek lamp shades / paying for friendships / based on how pornographic our breath smells.

I will not necessarily find myself / rationalizing / with computer gamers / and overly polite customer service robots / about how much life is lost on alternative realities / or how much violence the peaceful consumer causes.

The results of our language / cannot be programmed. / There is no proper way to hide the rampage / with whom we have been banking. / There are no words thick enough / to conceal the transparencies / in these stories I have crafted / out of loopholes and nothing but net.

The next life / is being offered to us daily / via livestreaming satellite / by entitled white rabbits / and tragedy addicts / dragging their fingernail / file / cabinets / across records of the damage my nerves have done.

Inglorious preachers of a sensational game, / sensations / and games / are at the root / of why we are walking so inefficiently, / warped 45s / with credit card swagger / charging up a sad sad path / like Ray Charles / singing "Seven Spanish Angels" / to the bottom of the barrel / in broad daylight.

Stop congregating in the valley / just because an echo / sounds good / when it agrees with itself. / A trajectory of misery / at this point / seems intentional. / We have all the information we need / to see clearly. / We are no longer toddlers / on the landscape of consciousness. / It is no longer cute / to crap ourselves. / Get the sticky off your buns / and roll with me. / No need for a night guard / if it still allows your jaw / to pulverize the truth.

The truth is / we feel fine. / Right now. / We are a point of complete / not a soundtrack / to the next life. / The future / gets no say / in who we are. / Thank you / for laughing / at the joke about sticky buns. / That was sweet. / This is nuts. / Optional. / Listen—

Having listened / to the parentheses of passive aggression / and made far too much bracket in response / incriminating ourselves / as sucker punches / and suckerfish / soaker hoses / and preying / on the dead weight / of fashion-forward food / for overpopulation—

Having inflicted the most amount of pleasure / with the least harm done / and called it progress, / I am still / without fail / eligible to remind us / that there is a reason / the future / gets so agitated / by our advances. / We are not built to barge ahead of ourselves / in false fast-forward / on a flat fifth wheel / made out of spokes people / for progress / who fly off the handle / whenever anyone taps the brakes.

Throw it in park. / Gauge the pressure. / Renunciation / is not a frigid concept. / It is okay / to abandon the tackle practice / of having and crashing / and having and crashing / through this circuit board of carrier pigeons / carrying torch carriers / over an orchestra of strung out sixteenth notes / composed with a matchstick / that struck out / and broke off / but did not burn up.

If the future / keeps finding us / in these uncomfortable positions /
they might mistake us for honest / before honest is actually true. /
How honest is it / that we drink / until we are dehydrated?

If my throat / turns to carbonated leather / and you hang me / like
a lucky foot / from the rearview mirror / while barreling down
the freeway / tollbooth after tollbooth / in a heavy glass ashtray /
wondering / how the hell freeways / got to be so goddamn expensive,
/ remember this—

The White Rabbit / is said to be a symbol / of human beings / who
are pompous and belittling / toward anything they deem less valuable
/ than themselves / yet they grovel / to accommodate anyone / from
whom they stand to gain.

To what end are you gaining? / I'm not speaking to our governments.
/ I'm speaking to the way / we govern ourselves. / Make your
stopwatch live up to its name. / We are not late for an important date.
/ We have simply shown up too early / for the next life / and forgot
to knock, / forgot / that the future / does not want us to arrive. / It
knows that if we do / it dies.

As if people on stilts / really need you to offer them more gravity.

THE GIFT OF MY HATE

At the Concert for New York City in Madison Square Garden, five
weeks after 9/11, Richard Gere stood in front of millions of viewers
and said:

We have the possibility to turn this horrendous energy
we are all feeling, from violence and revenge,
into compassion, into love, into understanding.

The crowd
    booed him
                                              loudly

as if to say,
    Hey!
    Buddha Boy,

We will not be caught dead acting like Jesus Christ.

As if Christ only published concepts he wanted us to thump
instead of experience.

Granted, *compassion* is a wounded word. It gets
banged around in the junk drawer. It is not an entitled
driver. Would not survive in California. Compassion
is often the last player picked. So maybe Richard Gere
should have used the word *rest* to suggest we curb the
poison of reacting so fast.

But journalists insisted Richard Gere's proposal for love and
understanding was the *wrong time, wrong crowd, wrong message.* I
remember being twenty-seven, watching this, feeling like some
fathers do not tell their children, *I am proud of you,* like an entire city
had learned the language of a well-disguised suicide, smothered in
clever headlines and a swarm of stagy news reporters who, years later,
failed to mention that a French man named Antoine Leiris lost his
wife, the mother of his child, with whom he was madly in love,

to the terrorist attacks in Paris the week before.
It was no more excruciating than what happened in
Baghdad, Beirut, or the West Bank
during the same twenty-four hours. The difference
is that five days later
Antoine Leiris was the only man
to post a love letter for his son on the BBC,
an open message to those responsible for killing his wife.
He looked directly into their hungry little pain-bodies
and told them,

I won't give you the gift of hating you.

                                              Pussy.

Pathetic propagandist.
      Candy-ass liberal. The insults
that followed Antoine's moment of peace made me
realize: *Love*—wounded a word as it may be—*Love*
can see *all of it, but* Anger, *anger is only concerned with what it
thinks is fair*, narrow like the barrel of the NRA,
like the blueprints to Russia's femininity,
to China's childhood, to North Korea's private parts,
to the bruised music of the Confederate flag states
still singing like a drunk Englishman
in a Tibetan monastery, loudly, louder, *Hey!*
I'm the Overcompensator!
                  The Great Annihilator!
Cross me and you will know my pain.

In each of us
          lives a
small man
      with a
good heart
      and an
ego the size of
          Hitler.

Why are we not fighting fire with water?
Compassion will not make us lazy. It is okay to cross
these borders. It is okay to stay awake,
to love our own ignorance enough to look it square in
the wise guy, in the bright side, at the parts we are
terrified to acknowledge because of the work it will
probably cause us,

because there is a chance we have been our own
terrorists. There is a chance we are a failed relationship.
There is a chance that every single day
we are the reason millions of animals actually
weep before slaughter, and we do not get to
make up for it by watching adorable YouTube
videos while stuffing our faces with their death.

It is more than some sellable cliché that—through these
bodies—we are rooted to the same source, that we have
arrived on this planet to experience form.
Now that we've had some time to do that, please,
let us reintroduce the idea of questioning, everything:

Excessive packaging. Planned obsolescence. Breeding... Planned
obsolescence. Identity... Planned obsolescence. Your story...
Planned obsolescence. The narrative... Planned obsolescence.
Your story. Your narrative. Your identity. Fining people... Planned
Obsolescence. Question anything impractical... Fining people,
because they didn't have enough money in the first place. Question
anything impractical to the eradication of suffering. Like denying
refugees. Like putting a fence around freedom. Like the oceans of
care we keep for this world getting so landlocked in our chest that
when the answer tries moving over all the God dams built across our
flooded hearts to surprise us with consciousness, it might look like
we are spitting back entitlements at the Earth.

Stand down. Stay still. Gather your wits. Find their ends.
    Pull out the slack and say clearly:

Yes.

Compassion.

Love.

Understanding.

Go ahead.
Call me another cliché.
Stick your violence in my meditation.
The worst you can do to me for not joining
the gangland war on Christ's behavior
is shoot me in the look on my face, the one that says,
I am not afraid to understand you. Or to stop you.

In *A New Earth*,
Eckhart Tolle refers to us as the noisiest humans
in history. Some things do not need to be fact-checked.
Stop backing up so loudly. You screaming sirens on a cell
phone. Heavy-footed upstairs neighbors.
Bloated bodies of anger belting out boos the size of
Madison Square Garden rejecting Richard Gere, who I
know very little about, but who I suspect, like most
humans, is part saint, part fraud, and who reporters had
to admit rebounded rather nicely when he acknowledged
that what he had to offer was
apparently unpopular right now—

Like taking away your child's assault rifle.
Like the color white. Like the color brown.
Like supporting the man in Nigeria
who found the cure for HIV.
Unpopular is compassion.
Like a savings account in Greece.
Like the topic of trafficking Stockholm Syndrome
all the way back from New York City
to right here down the west of me,
where I am determined to see all of it
because I don't get to go blind again,

not without carving the word *coward*
in holy braille
on every pen I will ever use
to point out how pain
cannot digest love.
It works the other way. My body
no longer loves writing poems for public consumption.
It does not believe in blowing apart.

But I am still right here behind its habits,
stacks of ground down teeth and a
mashed-up forehead of rolling credits, working
to see all of it,
which I suspect is more productive
than giving you

      the gift of my hate.

Did you not see the clock tower around my neck?

—**City**, to the people stuck in traffic

EVACUATION

I'd spent the last seven days, whenever my mind drifted, rereading that awful letter from memory, the one I'd sent to Steve, happy we were finally detached, navigating the pangs of my ungraceful dismount, thankful to be back at a center practicing seriously, done with the devastating distance of him. That's what I thought. That's what I was thinking when, around 1 p.m. on Day 7 of the Vipassana course in North Fork, a voice boomed throughout the room. I promise, if you sit in silence eleven hours a day for a week, and someone decides to address the room, any voice is booming:

Students. I need everyone's attention. There's a wildfire ripping through Yosemite headed this way and we've been informed that we have to evacuate the center as soon as possible.

All the students were gathered into the meditation hall. An effective impromptu rideshare system fell into place. A handsome, unassuming man named Clay was sitting on the mat just in front of me. We'd met briefly before the start of the course. I knew Clay had driven, so I leaned forward, *Hi Clay. As far as anyone knows I'm completely off the grid for another couple weeks. I've got nowhere to be but would like to head West. If you're headed that way, you can drop me off literally anywhere not on fire.*

Yeah man. You can ride with me.

Clay and I piled into his car. We shut the doors and looked at each other. For one moment—seven days long—we had been observing breath and sensations without reacting. In the next moment, we were senses floored, fast on the move out of the way of a wildfire. We both took a breath. Clay said we had to pick up one more person on our way out of the center, then he eased the car forward through a kind swarm of meditation students on the move.

Who are all these douchebags in our way? I asked, getting a feel for how far out Clay's humor would roll.

Yuh, get off my lawn, ya douche! Clay hollered.

Ha! Windows up. No one heard him. Thank goodness, on all accounts.

I don't remember the name of the woman who hopped into that car with us. She was old enough to be a big sister to my mother. We'll call her Wanda. There was field after passing field of fruit trees and other crops along the road to the right. Wanda was having trouble identifying some of them. The plants too. She sure wanted to know what each one was. She loved to talk of mundane things. I realized that if Clay dropped me off at an upcoming crossroads, I could hitchhike the rest of the way to camp with my 100-percenter Jon Berardi and his family. I'd never hitchhiked. I wanted to go for it. Clay squashed the idea. I'm thankful he did.

Of the two hundred plus Vipassana centers I mentioned, only eight or nine fully-operational centers were in the U.S. at the time. Of course, California has three of them. Of course Clay and I were within a few hours of another center. So, we decided to drive to the Vipassana center in Kelseyville, CA. We'd be arriving the night before Metta Day. Clay was very excited, because Metta Day is his favorite day at a Vipassana course. Metta Day is the day at the end of a ten-day course when new students learn to add the practice of love to their sits. For me, Metta Day is when I take all the clean energy I've generated throughout the course, all the love, and I share it. I let it travel outside myself, intentionally circulating it, opening the infinite resource of it, to the people sitting around me, to the whole room, throughout the grounds of the Vipassana center, to the town it's in, into the city, spreading, through the ground, all the way down to the other side of the earth, in every direction, into no ending whatsoever.

I was being pretty vocal with Clay and Wanda about the waves of precise coincidence I'd been experiencing, how clear the signs had become, of something greater. It was right then that Wanda began absentmindedly reading signs out loud. Signs, literally, beginning to identify every crop we passed. I laughed. A lightness spread through me, then beyond me. Moved water through my eyes when it did.

In the parking lot where we said goodbye to Wanda, Clay and I found a Thai restaurant. We sat there and took another breath.

Man, do you feel really emotional right now? I asked Clay.

He did. I can't claim to remember how it happened, but within a minute we were talking about sex addiction. Maybe I'd mentioned how clear my reception was, not just from the last seven days of sitting, but from maintaining sīla as well. I leaned in, *I've been celibate for two and a half months. Not even my hand.*

Clay was kind and hilarious in the way he supported me before revealing he'd practiced celibacy for two and a half years, prior to meeting his girlfriend.

What?! Is that real?

METTA DAY

Clay and I made it safely to the Vipassana Center in Kelseyville, CA, found our rooms and settled in. Clay was already in the kitchen meeting the other volunteers the next morning before I turned up. One of the servers asked Clay who was with him. Clay told her he didn't know much about me, except that I was a poet thinking about moving to Los Angeles.

When I got to the kitchen that day, Metta Day, the server who'd asked Clay about me approached and introduced herself. *Hi, I'm Lexi. I heard you're a poet. I was once on the Pittsburgh Poetry Slam team.* We talked about people we both might know then Lexi said, *I heard you're thinking of moving to L.A. I don't know if you're interested, but I've been meditating about it for the last ten days and I'm looking for someone to take over the lease on my apartment. It's in Los Feliz. A thousand dollars a month. I want someone there by September. The only catch is that I'm thinking of going to Peru and never coming back, so I can't take my things. It's furnished already. Dishes, bed, bookshelves, air conditioner, all yours. There's a view of the Hollywood sign and the Griffith Park Observatory.*

No doubt about it. I let Lexi know that, even though I was already a shoo-in, I'd have a look at the place on July 19th. A friend of mine from Australia, Carl, was coming for a stateside visit so we could explore Yosemite, and I was to meet him first in L.A. The flight was already booked.

To also discover a cathedral with stained glass lit up at night, just outside my window, as part of the view of the Hollywood Hills, and that I was a block and a half between two meditation centers, was too much to not start laughing for what must have looked like no reason at all.

WHICH ONES?

After Metta day, Vipassana centers clear out to make room for the next crew of folks scheduled to meditate. This happens year-round. It's about a three-day turnaround for cleaning, restocking, food prep and a ton of other logistics focused on the needs of the incoming students. At that point, I'd been visiting Vipassana centers in some capacity for ten years. This was the only time I was at a center where—instead of tending to logistics—everyone left, except for two people who hadn't planned to be there: Guadalupe and me.

Guadalupe had traveled up to the area from Mexico to snip bud for extra money. Partway through the job she recognized her environment as toxic and opted to find a Vipassana center for the rest of her stay. I was supposed to still be five hours away in North Fork.

What a lovely time to be with Guadalupe and her smile in the kitchen prepping food for 120 people. Her English was just good enough that we could make a joke when we didn't understand what the heck the other was saying. Her incredible smile, like it was still learning itself.

Before it was down to just Guadalupe and me, there was also Cha-Zay. Cha-Zay was interested in a real estate purchase nearby, then enjoying the day at a rumored nearby watering hole we never found. It was a lovely lunch with Cha-Zay. We talked about the tiny home community I'd been dreaming up. We looked at a property or two. We drove around in search of a watering hole. Cha-Zay told me about her three near-death experiences, and the book she wrote called, *I'm Dying: Shit! Not again!* So, I asked what she knew about aliens. Cha-Zay asked, *Which ones?*

Aisle 5. Bottom left.

—**Marbles**, explaining where they can be found

THE DAY THE GAYS WON MARRIAGE

Even though my flight wasn't scheduled to leave California back to Boulder for another week, I left the Kelseyville Vipassana center early. I'd smashed my hand at the gym a couple weeks prior, and it wasn't getting any better. It needed to heal up.

I thought it would be fun to make my way down to Alameda and stay with Jon Berardi now that he and his family were back from their camping trip. A woman at the Kelseyville center was headed down to Petaluma that day. Of course Sarah Healy's home is in Petaluma. Sarah Healy, you know, the ocean-swimming mother of women with big feet who said, *The lesson / will be repeated / until you learn it.*

Sarah was out of town, but told me where the key was.

On our way.

During the drive, I opened my phone for the first time in days to see social media fireworks flying for legal love.

I spent the night meditating at Sarah's with Jasper the Cat purring snug in my lap. Took a bus to Oakland the next day for a surprise reunion BBQ with the Kagan-Trenchards and crew. Their son, Gideon, his hug brought tears to me. He would not let go until I settled down.

Of course Anis was in town. Revival. We slept in a Berkeley hilltop home with a view of the Golden Gate Bridge. We took a train to San Francisco Pride the next morning. I met up with 100% Joe. We celebrated, then I dipped out to catch a train in time for dinner with the Berardis. On the way from 100% Joe to 100% Jon, there was a clearing in the crowd and a view of the city.

When I tell you there was a clearing, what I mean is that I was walking through the epicenter of San Francisco Gay Pride and noticed that about fifty yards in front of me, and about fifty yards behind me, there was no one but me. I heard an instrument and stood still. It was a man playing "Pachelbel's Canon" on a stringed harmonic lap piece. Goose bumps grew from my ears. Joe and Jon and I met exactly twenty years ago at a camp in Indiana. We were on the same team. They played "Pachelbel's Canon" at the graduation. They played "Pachelbel's Canon" at every single graduation I ever worked there, fourteen years. That camp, where they asked me what I would do if I knew I couldn't fail. In a post on Facebook the next day, I wrote:

The Berardis left yesterday for Indiana. I am in their new home babysitting Sherbet the Hamster until my flight leaves. Summer Thanksgiving here all week long. If you caught my post a couple months ago about the hitchhiker I picked up in Oregon, 1,000 miles away from where I met her last year, you can appreciate that of course we crossed paths again yesterday. We ate Thai food in the shade and paid attention. She's on her way to Mount Shasta with her new gold dog, K, named after my tour manager, Kaylen. Of course she needed a ride to Muir Beach. Of course that's where I first said the words, You're amazing for the things you see, *to Jon Berardi, as Joe ran laps on the horizon line. Of course the hitchhiker and I took a selfie and touched the ocean.*

THE REQUEST

Soon after I arrived in Boulder I got an email from a woman named Jenna in NYC asking if she could commission me to write a poem for her sister's wedding. I wasn't sure I wanted the job.

After much consideration about the best way to spend my energy post-tour, knowing that my editing process is often an obsessive child, I agreed to speak with Jenna on the phone to find out more about the couple, Robyn and Matt, and decide whether or not they were a poem I could be excited to write. It occurred to me that drawing from the love I once had might serve as a healthy exercise in letting go. I just had to make sure the story of the couple wasn't criminally dull.

When on the phone, I generally jump straight to the point. I don't remember the pleasantries exchanged, but we dove pretty quickly into the history of Robyn and Matt. I know because I remember the approximate length of time it took for me to decide whether or not I could create a poem worthy of their marriage. It went like this:

Jenna said, *They met because it was raining at a festival and they were both struck by the same lightning—*

I'm in.

The Gospel of Lightning

What paper planes and empty seats
most have in common
is that they are best made by children
still learning how to ride things out.

There is a lot to be said for practice.
And propellers. Don't sit down for this. Not yet.
Everything in turn until we become invisible
like a death–do–us–part party, and even then—

Dear Big Britches and Elbow Grease, ride with me.
Sleeves up. Top down. Wild–eyed and astronomical.
The balance of being young
still creasing into our laughter lines.
Let everyone else refer to themselves as an old soul
if that's what they need to smile.

But we, the awe-stricken and lightning-struck,
we know better. Every moment is a brand new baby,
Baby. Every vow is a brave new voice. Thank goodness
your voice still calls me Home. And Work.
And Pickle Sticks. As in, *What in the hell did you*
say that for, Pickle Sticks?

Please, let this life be proof we are working
for the indestructible source of Yes. We are paid
well in the ways we arrive at each other,
and we rest, knowing everything is easy in orbit,
not just the sun, Sunny Buns. This day too.

Let every last one of our days be proof
that *Don't stop accepting* is our only instruction
because *We won't stop changing* is the only truth.

The truth is

this universe is gassy and unpredictable.
It still has not said excuse me for the Big Bang.
Sometimes we expect too much
instead of practicing enough
or receiving in us just the right answer. You,
the staggering answer. The truth

is that there is very little difference
between a brilliantly written horoscope
and a baby mobile shaped like the Milky Way.
And there is a day for every last star
with exactly the same outcome—

Us

falling asleep, side-by-side
in our primetime pillow-talk show,
maps to the music of midnight,
while the rest of the world goes static en masse, magically
marked in firefly parts across cinematic patches of
looking glass. Look—

I do not know if I will be able to make you happy
on the eighth day of our seventeenth year
or on the fourth month of our third decade
because I've never been that far.
But you can know for sure I am already doing my best.
You will always have my best.
You are the home I point to that lives in my chest.

It's true.

What children and the landing of a plane
most have in common, is that they are best made
by a line drive of pilot lights guided
through a single tambourine,
across the day we met in a field of wet
metal hands
on the Gospel of Lightning.

WE ARE IN THE SNACK!

When I'm with my nephew and little cousins
I understand that I was not wired to have children
as an evolutionary protection
to keep my heart from bursting. A piano stampede.
Sweet barreling daylight. You honey-buttered
roll models, the molecular structure of miracles
was never anything but the truth.

Years ago, when they were your age,
I told Joe and Avery Whipple that chickens were dumb.
The next day I told them a story about how Garth,
our dead rooster, threw himself between a
coyote and the coop to protect the hens.
Ten-year-old Joe looked mad at me,
like a man of his word would, and said,
I thought you told us chickens were dumb.

The day after that, we hiked up to the snow in the
mountains. When Avery's dad asked if she wanted a
snack, eight-year-old Avery grabbed a handful of
snowcap, crammed it into her mouth and yelled,
Dad! We're in the snack!

Nephew, cousins, don't you forget it. You
bounce castle billionaires. You holy hymnal anthems.
You choir of honest killers. It is okay to be a man like
Joe. It is okay to be a woman like Avery. To be both
at the same time. Some people

will start each day by stepping out of their homes
like they were being forced to burn them, or clean them,
or eat a wet lemon sandwich. *Anything can happen*,
they will say, and they will say it sour,
like *anything* is a crabby apple babble cake with
too much crabby babble. *Those* people

will create brotherhoods and sisterhoods and
neighborhoods out of locks and gates
and a million silly reasons to own a gun that have nothing
to do with feeding you. Help is on the way.
You have always been on the way.

Keep company with whom happiness is never in
question. Look at this world that is yours.
A festival of party lights hanging
all the way around the horizon line.
You will be so glad you did not sleep on the chance
to stay strung up 'til dawn, talking about life
with your best friend, even when Mom makes you
roof the house hungover. The hammering home.

Come to Uncle Buddy's when the job is done.
We'll talk so much shit on that woman
she'll smell your breath from where we're sitting
underwater, sipping tea in the pool out back. But at least
she will know you made it to me safely.
Love her for that. She would be eaten by the coyotes for
you. She already has. You just don't know it yet.
I'm proud of you for fixing the roof.

A time *will* come when you can spend entire weeks
eating toast in bed and answering to no one.
I promise. Work. Live for a living.
That's different than leaving for a living.
Keep your patience. Let the otters photobomb every
graduation, all tomorrow's parties, and the whales.
The whales. Breeching. If the landscape

ever feels too beautiful to bear, remember to remember
that you can't sink your teeth into everything.
Hand off the sink to an astronaut thought. Let it lift you
higher. Stay up. You balloonatics. My fat-cheeked top-
of-the-mornings. Be gentle with yourselves. Don't get so
disappointed in your failures that you fail to celebrate
their honesty. Of course you failed. You're doing it right.

Love yourself, this much, as much as all the teachers
who ever dreamed of teaching you when they were still
dreaming of becoming teachers. Before the color red.
Before they stayed inside. Outside of the Earth itself
it may look like the shadow of a hang glider is the only
thing that can move a mountain. But I've seen trains
chugging through the side of the rock.
I've seen who builds them. It's not a miracle.

Miracles are just constant recurring reminders
of how much we forget to pay attention.
You have the most important jobs of all: to remind us
to notice everything. The words we fell in love with,
like *elastic* and *sober* and *able* and *west*
and *with*, and *with*, and *You taught taught me a lot lot
honey honey. Thank you*

and *I'm sorry* are the gateway words to vulnerability.
Vulnerability is what made every movie, sang every song,
and wrote every poem that ever plugged a life back into
itself. Don't be embarrassed to save the world. In Iceland
there are over one hundred words for *wind*.

Anything can happen, you definite greenlights.
You happily-ever-afters. Anything at all. Except
for achieving a level of Christmas sweater game
as tight as mine, sweet child, it is not a skill
that can be taught, but you may touch them.
Be touched by this life, by the softest reasons we're in it,

by the pink and the blue and the way this world is
sometimes too much lonely, a bankruptcy of sky.
The only way out is out. Lead us out. You are not alone.
I will remind you as often as you need me to.
It is my favorite thing to do, you extraordinary daylight
cartoon dynamite, you bumbling tumblehome,
jumbo wagon laugh, lovers of the dinner bell ringing.
You hippopotamus rex.

Somewhere, there's a chicken in a snowsuit who made it
out alive asking the two most important questions
anyone ever asked: *To what end?*
And *Why are you calling me names?*
Be a hand raised high in the answer. Be a head held high
in the smoke. The enlightenment. The practice of it,
of home is who you are. The next time

I get to be with you in November, the week we
go around the circle saying what we're thankful for,
I can hardly wait to not shut up.

Up. Sand. Hands. Grass. Being naked. Sisal rugs. Rubs.
A hardwood stage. Gas pedals. The street. Walking away from
a tragedy. The pursuit of love for life on my teeth.

—**Feet**, listing their favorite things

Bois D'Arc

David Murphy knew he was going to die. So he did.

It took a very long time.

My best friend could not stop bleeding.

I don't want it to take so long.

I've had to let him go. But not the love.

We get to keep that.

Take as long as you need. I'll be in the car.

My foot weighs seventy-four-miles-per-hour.

Thirty-nine in a thirty-five. Compassion

has to keep the same momentum as impermanence

if you really want it to work. Effort

is the friction of intent.

I intend to make it past the aftermath of beauty

the day it got mistaken for perfect.

I can't believe you didn't know you were beautiful.

Heret Herot

It's not that I don't like you, it's that you don't.
I'm just following your lead.

When you came to me with your worth,
put it in my hands,
and asked me how to read it,

it was like watching Jesus
ask if I still believed in Him
just because He flipped a table.

Your body remembers the soundtrack to your past life.
It remembers the next life coming.

Some things
you don't have to ask.

Don't be scared of the voice in your head
that's kindly been calling you God,

even if it reads like a map to the Minotaur,
written on rats in wine.

Luckily,
dignity, like a lung, is regenerative
if you stop sucking tar pits into it.

One day, we'll look back on all this pain
like a parent we were obligated to love.

You'll be glad you did.
Love each one.

Don't suffer until you have to.
Pay attention and you won't have to.

Blacklisting your thoughts
is resistance.
I've been trying to soften the blow

instead of giving you what you asked for,
the truth about our death.

Stop asking me what you're worth.
You're worth a million bucks
in the hole of a shallow man's pocket,

masquerading as depth,
grand marshal of the strength charade,
as I sometimes find you to be.

Every encounter you've ever had
has been a performance.

I don't get to say these things
without seeing them first in myself.
You saw the worst in yourself

and carried it around like a baby
nursing the end of a candle
I'd been saving for a cannon to fire you from.

It was a war I fought with hope,
the hope you would lighten up,

the palm I planted on the soft spot
when you were coming in over my head in a fuss
struggling to learn surrender.

The day I gave my life to Jesus
I attempted to speak in tongues.

I opened my mouth and out came out:
Heret Herot. Heret Herot.

Twenty years later,
I asked if anyone knew what that meant.

My nephew said, *I do.*
It means, "How we fought. How we fought."

When I woke up,
I searched to find out for myself.
The first thing I read was this:

Heorot, also Herot, is a mead-hall
described in the epic, Beowulf,
as the foremost of halls under heaven.

Heorot means "Hall of the Hart."
Beowulf defends the royal hall and its residents
from Grendel.

Grendel was a creature of darkness,
exiled from happiness, accursed of God,
devourer of humankind,

loved candlelit wildfires,
long walks across the face of your safety,
has become the way you see yourself.

If wanting to save the world from the way it sees itself
signifies a savior complex,
you nailed me.

My friends all go by Beowulf,
so I need it for your death to be done,

the tragedy, the dead weight,
the talking points you've used
to strengthen your grief.

I don't remember who's dead and who isn't.
I just know you're not.

I'm only telling you what I saw:
an exact cross
between everyone I've ever had a crush on.

It makes me feel, more than I'm willing to,
so I can't guarantee a rounded response,

but here I am at the foot of your labyrinth
trying to speak to you in a language
a lot less vague than tongues:

When someone tells you they love you, believe them.
Expect them to read the book of your life
in best-case scenario.

Some people know what to kill while they're dying.
So they do. Turn off the gas light.

If anyone tries to convince you
that your intuition is false, confront your attacker.
Take your worth back. It's not my book.

Just because people don't call you on your bullshit
doesn't mean they don't see your bullshit.

None of us have enough experience yet
to deal with the work that is still up to you.

There are consequences
for the good we think we're doing
when we doubt ourselves for being alive.

My love: You are the Minotaur. You've just forgotten.
Me: I know, but …
My love: They are yours to devour.

The Nines

Two things you need to know for this story to make sense:

1) I performed a love poem written for Steve at a venue called Town Hall in Seattle, Washington, with The Seattle Orchestra in front of eight hundred people including most anybody who was a player in the relationship between us. I nailed it. Not the relationship, the poem.

2) When I first moved in with Steve, he wanted me to see a movie he'd already seen called *The Nines*, starring Ryan Reynolds and Melissa McCarthy, about a man living three parallel realities, each being unaware of the other. The theme of the movie is to *Look for The Nines*. Look for the other people bringing consciousness into all this content. When the movie was over, Steve told me he thought I was a nine. I was flattered. *Don't mind if I am.*

The Nines occasionally came to mind throughout our relationship, but nothing overtly happenstance, unless you count the time we played touch football with Ryan Reynolds at a mutual friend's wedding. Who does that? We did. I was on Ryan's team. And Ryan stopped Steve from getting two touchdowns, which was its own beautiful sight. I had actually never seen Steve so... springy.

The week I left Steve, I was walking down the long, dark proverbial tunnel to the light. It's in Port Townsend, Washington. Fort Worden. I was literally walking down a long, dark tunnel, making my way to the light. At the end of the tunnel, where the light began, was a metal pole sticking up from the ground to prevent vehicles from coming and going. When I walked out of the tunnel, I saw that someone had written on the pole in black Sharpie, *LOOK FOR THE NINES*.

On May 25, 2017, I was renovating my apartment and received an uncharacteristic message from Steve that finally caused me to remove the possibility of us getting back together. I wrote him back. Two sentences. Four words each. It doesn't matter what they said because, out of context, it wouldn't make sense. It mattered only to the rescue effort of my dignity. The point is, after nearly three and a half years of trudging through the indecision of us, I finally made my peace and disconnected from the disconnect. When I hit *Send* on those final words, I shut the computer, stood up, and literally felt the anger and the resentment pop like a tapioca pearl, fizzing out of my body. The relief immeasurable. The hugest smile, from my chest up, eyes watery in the lightness of being. And the Fuck yes.

That day, I got an email from Town Hall in Seattle. They were about to undergo a year of renovations and wanted to confirm my participation in a show they were throwing called Town Hall's Last Hurrah. It would have been the week of Steve's and my seventh anniversary. They were paying me the exact amount of money I lost when I had gone back to Seattle at the end of the world tour. And they wanted me to open for *Seattle's most requested party band*, The Nines.

DANNY SHERRARD

Sometime in 2012, Danny Sherrard texted me, excited about opening for one of his favorite bands in Seattle. Something happened at the last minute that excluded Danny from opening the show and he was deflated. I was too. Ever the good sport, Danny texted, *There was a door by the river.* I immediately began to write a new piece, born of his abstract optimism. There was a door by the river. It's taken seven years to finish it, the last piece to be completed for this book, in fact.

Recently, I wrote Danny to let him know that I took his random text as a prompt all those years ago. Danny let me know our friend, C.R. Avery, had written it. If you've heard "The Information Man," from my last book, *Stunt Water,* you can imagine how much this pleased me.

I've never been so intimidated to complete a poem, it constantly daring me to fail the goddamn math class it was offering. Even in sending this book to the editors, this poem was still undone.

When Steve and I started dating, we would email daydreams back and forth about what our life together might look like. There were seven daydreams. In 2010, I wrote a love poem called "In Landscape" that would one day be performed at Seattle's Town Hall with a band called The Nines. In it, I ask Steve to *meet me by the eighth daydream, in the wide-open purpose of a locomotive coming to a standstill with the sea.* That feels like an important note as you move into the next poem.

Boy: *How are rocks formed?*
Man: *Some people just get tired of being wrong, so they stop learning.*

Boy: *Where did you learn that?*
Man: *I was a mountain once.*

WE BECOME MOUNTAINS

1.
There was a door by the river
it is still standing still where we found it
jammed in the ground
astonished
by a lack of traffic
appealing to the day they say the accident happened
while he was driving home
the point
was in the passenger's seat
busted up
from holding up
its head against the window on the door

by the river

there were two chains hanging from a tree branch
with no seat in between
for a mood to sit
and connect its swing
finally
the relief of removing his wrung-out hands
from the wreckage of the weakest link
these
things change
and there's nothing wrong with the way of rust
how it spreads outside the velocity
of all this keeping up.
Keep up.
If your breath gives out take another

once

there was a driver with a hunger for love
when it leaves
home
hidden in the heart of his house
with a photo
of a pack of matches
balanced
on the ledge of his watering mouth
crying
We become mountains
scalloped in the floors of daybreak
buried in the landscape
breathing like an epitaph bearing the words

by The River

2.
there was a writer who was wrecked in his heart
from the start
who wrote a lot
he could not take back
drafts
scribbled
on a stack of detailed oil rag maps
along the travel path of action and lights
lit up
from the match he struck
on the welcome mat
and ran it against the wind.
It is okay to ask for directions
if the fireworks are leading back to accidents
over and over and over again
burning
in the what-it-takes of staying awake
when everything blows up in your world at

once

there was a silver compass covered
in elbow grease
pointing dizzy at the dirty south
bound
train trust
saving up for traction
north
true to chugging like a drunk mole
digging for the gold
mine
buried in a landslide run-on sentence
recently released
from being haunted
by the high-speed dirty reverse
of the events that led to the neglect that crashed
and burned in the driving thirst

by the river

3.
there were two lovers laying by a door to the sea
that had snaked its way
through town
on a river of reminders
of a locomotive's imminent
impasse
with the ocean's mouth
exactly where the railings on the bridge washed out
side
sweeping down the coast
cleared clean
into the seam of the eighth daydream
awoke
to winding around the bend
where there was nothing ever brighter
than the knowing what was gone
had passed the point of ever coming back to die again
once

there was a fighter pilot cleared to take the whole day off,
skywriting out his name in the blue blue
blue
jet
stream stretches
over every new beginning
to a story
at end of the line
drive
left
fields
carried away from the loss
he caused
when he was driving all the blood through hell,
a drive you won't see him blaming on anyone else
caught out loud singing how
We become mountains
scalloped in the floors of daybreak
buried in the landscape
breathing like an epitaph bearing the words

by The River

You think I don't want to turn over?

—**Engine**, exhausted

ALARMING LAZINESS

It started with double cheeseburgers. After being a vegetarian for years, I simply couldn't shake the idea of eating a double cheeseburger, mouth watering with the ghost of double cheeseburgers past. So I ate one. One from nearly every restaurant within delivery distance of Los Feliz. There was no shame, for the first couple weeks. And, before I got lazy, there was express thanks to each cow. Five months of them. Twenty pounds of them. My body demanding to ground. The truth is, it started with fish. Fish is the gateway food to double cheeseburgers. My double cheeseburgers wanted company. Fries and a shake. Yes, I will have the pie. The cookies, the soda, and an embarrassing amount of mayonnaise. All the greazy table napkins. We should get BBQ with mac & cheese and beans and sweet potatoes. What's the place with all the bells and the tacos? Order it. Be alone with it. Don't leave the house. Get it delivered. I'm in the middle of Season 72. And pot. That'll stop the thinking and make it feel better and let my stomach hold more so I can get a bigger shovel. Before you bring the shovel put sushi on it. Put garlic bread and ravioli. Thai with a side of peanut sauce. This is so easy. This feels so good. *What the hell are you doing? Not having a weird relationship with food. Why?* Take a break, buddy. Remember the time you wanted to rest? You're doing that, and there's no one to stop you, from shooting past level one thousand on Candy Crush. Do not tell people you played a thousand levels of Candy Crash, you fat fuck. You lazy twat. You blubbery whale. Don't forget to feel no shame. This is just a graduation in the middle of saying goodbye to instant gratification. The spirit world wants us back. Two years of resistance is too long gone. Let's make our way back, as soon as we finish this book. Treat yourself. Every single day. Until it piles to the top of your throat. Until your gut busts and your bank account gives out. Get it together, boy. You were born to back up what you say. Stop saying it. Back up.

I Was a World Tour

There's never been a time when I've not lived
in consideration of my ideal self, writing toward him,
hoping to one day fill that man's shoes.

When I was forty, I took a shit in a house that poetry
paid for and wondered if I was still a fool.

Intention must have counted for something.

In seventh grade, I prayed for wisdom while taking a shit
and crying about how much pain I was in for wanting a
man to live in my body instead of the suffering and the
puppy and the girl who did.

I took us all on a world tour in shoes that kept falling off.

THE LIKELY SALOON

On the Night Kite Poetry Revival Tour, Timmy Straw,
Derrick Brown, Anis Mojgani, and myself stopped for
gas in a town called Likely, CA.
It was an antique pump. There was a saloon next door.
The Likely Saloon. Derrick and Timmy wanted to go in.
We did. Timmy got carded.

There was a man with bare feet and a violin.
He was a hitchhiker. Four men sat at the bar. The owner
was the bartender. Timmy found a piano in the
backroom by the pool table. She and the violinist
fiddled around for a minute. The owner
came by to watch. Timmy played a song she
wrote called "Gethsemane." The boys and I,
we love that song. We sang along. We couldn't help it.
Then we saw the owner weeping.

He asked if we wanted to stay in his guest room
so we didn't have to drive all night. We had to drive all
night. We listened to ourselves on the radio. We buckled
to the ground in laughter, seeing who could throw the
biggest rock in the river, pretending it really mattered.

I smoked a joint on the side of a circus tent
in Glastonbury. A woman named Evanson was there
and we were wearing our Wellies. We got work and
flew to Banff. We lived in a motion picture.
It won an award for having some style about it.
I danced at the Roxi in Amsterdam. I met a man.
We bounced street lights off the canal. We kicked a
sandcastle into the air. We read poems to it and ran off.
I'll sit at the kids table. You ain't gotta tell me twice.
Hell no. I didn't come here to live two times.
I'll go as quietly as a loud man can.

We burned a couch in the middle of the soccer field,
stumbled to the center line, laughing. We set it on fire,
laughing. We ran from the police, laughing.
We burned a couch in the front yard. We burned a
couch in the woods at The Woody.
Somebody brought acid and a blow-up doll. We had a fat
plastic bat and some ground rules. We used the keg for
second base. I wore a Hawaiian button-up. Monster
Magnet blasted from the floodlight. From the
theater kids. It is impossible for fun to regret itself.

So we tackled through the snow in Central Park.
We slept in the clock tower above New York City.
We floated down the river and made a pyramid out of
gay people. We threw a double-decker
bus party. We read poems from the top of a
lifeguard shack in the wind on Long Beach.
We read poems on the bow of the Queen Mary.
We played xylophones to the ghosts. We stood in the
dock lights. Somewhere in the ocean was a fog machine.

We read poems to the staff after the bar closed in Maine.
The jazz musicians next door to Stonewall asked if I
wanted to read a poem. I asked if a bear shits anywhere it
wants to. I didn't come here to say no. You ain't gotta ask
me twice. I took adult gymnastics just to throw myself
across the trampolines, just to flip into the foam.
I slipped on a banana peel. The ground gave way. White
water rafted. The bed we broke in Tucson. The bronze
microphone we poured by the fire in Arcosanti.

People smiled about the way I loved them.
Me and David Murphy were asked to leave the tent,
three hours after I told him the joke about why dogs lick
their balls. It was our first time getting high.
I got to be in this world while David was still in it.
James too. We floated the bayou on Styrofoam boats.
We smoked a joint with Bret outside the rehab.

We read poems in a convenience store. We gathered
$150 for the cashier, to help with her third job. We held
up the train with water guns and made people take
compliments. No one was hurt. We scared people with
our love. I stood on a stool at Stanford to defend a boy
practicing his team cheer in the cafeteria. When the
wrestling camp intimidated him to stop, we kept going.
The whole cafeteria rose to the occasion. I ate meals with
comedians. I swallowed food from Italy. I cleaned my
plate. We cleaned the van. We danced in a fountain
with Spring Arbor. Lake Forest. Sanborn, NY.

We played music in Surfside until the car battery died.
We walked home through the sand dunes. With
flashlights. Kealoha sang to us under the waterfall. I grew
an ivy down to the ground from the ceiling of my
apartment. I played Emancipator to help it along. I
whispered Peace into the water jug and knew what I was
doing. I don't feel like I've wasted any of these lives.

We read poems to two Santa Clauses at the same time in
a basement in Scotland. We read poems to San Quentin
'enitentiary. To Laramie, Wyoming. To the
rn lights in Iceland. At every outdoor festival. In
with Thuli and Page. We read poems at rock
ts every night for years. To the tour bus snacks.
1an asked me to sign her boobs.

d the times. I high dived. I skydived. I duck dove.
ode. I leaned into it, y'all. I've seen a million faces.
ot rock them all. I double-dipped my bread sticks,
y the opposite ends. We saw the world. We
Niagara fell. Into the beer at the Sydney Opera House.
Into the city behind it, alive. We sailed to Tazmania. We
took the ferry to Kingston. I jogged through Wales.
Through Brighton. I escaped from Alcatraz. We made
the front page.

I watched Andrea Gibson perform "Thank Goodness" with their bare hands. I read "Church of the Broken Axe Handle" until I no longer felt alone. Derrick sang a Journey song to the people in the Mexican restaurant with his chest hair. He was laying on the hood of the van. We did donuts in the parking lot. Anis was wearing a glow-in-the-dark money sign necklace. I was a considerate boy.

I held the door open at the deli and got free bologna. I hid in the corn fields and spent my allowance down at the dairy. We flew to Puerto Vallarta and jumped in naked. I saw a kid there dance like he was supposed to. No one was watching. There were windmills and cobblestone outside The Blow Hound. I know because we read poems to them. I walked through the Hall of Mosses with a flockprinter. Flockprinter.

Sometimes I stayed home and ate cereal. I caught grapes in my mouth with precision. And almonds. We all saw the poems we wrote live their happiest lives on stage. Not everything up here is acting. People printed us on their bodies. I don't have any tattoos, but I remember all one thousand steps to the top of Nafplion. I spotted the whale shark. I played fetch with Lucy in an ocean. Every Frisbee Tucker caught in the sky. None of us cared about the lightning. We knew what we were getting into. Every acid sunrise. The whiplash from the laughing when we landed.

I prayed for us in Monemvasia. In all the cathedrals. My two best friends were geese. The Colonel and Mrs. Marple. We loved our home. They rode in the back seat. We wore shoes with wheels in the heels. We rolled to the rings by the pier. My name was on the marquee under a quote about love, how it makes no mistakes. Everybody loved the show. The helicopters above Los Angeles, braided through the sky. The Griffith Park Observatory. I loved a man.

We bought a house once. We put it in the woods. I built
a mosaic water feature out of seventeen different colors.
There were three ponds and a teak guest bed for Bob.
There was a black bear who got drunk on fermented
plums. He didn't want no trouble. Nobody ever did.
I collected enough sea stones to draw us a daydream. We
threw the end-of-summer party. We passed out brownies
and cold bottles of dance until daylight. There was green
grass on our side. We woke up in it.

We cleaned up nice. Sometimes there was money in our
pocket. We had friends in high places. They sang songs
about us. I read poems with gospel singers. With an
orchestra. With Georgia. I read a poem to monks. With
Saul. With Sage. With Ani. In New Orleans. In Alaska.
On the slope. The dogsleds. The frozen river.
With the bagpipes. In a kitchen at a hostel in Dublin.
I earned a free room that night.

We saw the landscape and listened to its opinion on
being still. We rolled down the hill through the brambles
at Gas Works Park. Seattle forever. Best friends forever.
The Dares forever. I read a poem called "Cannonball
Man" to a Canadian border guard. It was the first time he
smiled in his whole life. I swear.

I saw the second largest sunflower ever grown. I won an
Easter raffle with the number eight. I met the same
hitchhiker four times. We touched the ocean with a
golden retriever. There was a hot spring hole in
Yosemite, alone on a massive plain. Somebody left a joint
for us. We got naked again and stayed a while. We could
see clear across the field. Across the stars. We read poems
to The Green Mill. At Lowlands, under the acrobats.

I did all the drugs. I ran to the top of a lighthouse
and slid the whole way down it with Leigh. We could
not stop laughing. Leigh drove us all the way home. I
worked hard to look this old. I burned both ends, bright
as I could. Before my hair turned white in the spotlight.
In the lovers. All my lovers. Any anger has turned away
from me now. It cost too much. We got what we asked
for the van. Kaylen gave me expensive creams.

It has been worth living to have had these friends. To
have had this tour. This dynamite tour. This incredible
life. We read poems to the moment we were here at the
same time. We paid in full. We called dibs on The Likely
Saloon. We sang backup. You ain't gotta tell us twice.
We lived long enough to know where our voices landed.
And our jokes. A bed of leaves. There were so many
fields and forests. Good people came from them. It's true
what they said we did. We worked for it. We drove all
night. We read poems to each other. Wells on the violin,
laughing.

Timmy played "Gethsemane."

You are welcome here.

—Home

Armageddon with Mom

Last Thanksgiving Eve, 2018, Mom asked where she could find me when it all goes down. Like, society collapsing kinda shit. Fair enough.

I guess I'd go home.

What I meant was, *To Steve's house.* It took us both by surprise. It had been a year and a half since we spoke, and nearly five years since I walked out.

We met at Seattle Gay Pride in 2010. I was waiting in a line for the Honey Buckets, fifty folks deep. Steve walked over and asked me to hold his beer so he could fish the phone from his sock, because he doesn't like keeping things in his pocket, but he was going to get my number. Even drunk and stumbly, Steve's symmetry was a thing to behold. Beautiful. Beast.

By the time we reached the toilets it was decided that I'd buy his best friend's half of their house when the time was right, then move in so we could get on with it.

I'd been talking to an Air Force captain named Kurt all day. Things were progressing nicely with Kurt, mostly because he was an awful man, so I returned to him after I left the outhouse and didn't see Steve. A minute later, no warning, Steve stepped in, said, *I'm just running interference.* As in, *I can't let this happen. He's with me.* There was a pregnant pause. I think everyone felt awkward in it but me. I was too busy falling in love. With Steve. And that's how it started. He stole me up.
No one's ever felt as safe as I did then.

After I let Mom know where she could meet me in the end times, I wrote Steve a letter then sat on it for three weeks. Every time I tried to send it, I'd stop myself. And each time I stopped myself, you guessed it, some sweet chance thing occurred. For example, the first time I withheld the letter, I closed my computer, left the apartment to grab dinner, and saw this leaned up against a wall outside:

On the sixth time in three weeks of sitting on the letter, I closed
my computer and didn't send it again, opened Instagram. I'd been
tagged on a post by a woman I didn't know. She had a giant octopus
tattooed on the right side of her body. Same as Steve. In researching
details to verify claims, I discovered the tattoo is actually on her left
side. But, to be fair, the picture was taken in a mirror. And if Mom
had been doing the research, she would've pointed out, *It wadn't an
octopus. It was a snake.*

When I wrote to the woman to make sure I had it right, she said, *I do
not have an octopus on my hip, but a wet snake wrapped around the skull of a
señorita. She looks like an octopus though. Almost as if she was trying to be one.*

Not mentioned, but unmistakably, Señorita wears a rose as big as
her skull.

In my hunger for connection, I sent the letter. Steve didn't get it. I'd
accidentally sent it to an old email address he used when we owned a
landscaping company.

No problem. After eighteen months of not seeing or speaking to each other, Stephen decided to call me that week anyway.

We must have walked fifteen miles when he came to visit that
month. We were good to each other. And for each other. That hadn't
happened in a long time.

On the walk from Los Feliz to Echo Park Lake, all the blocks that
had lived in our relationship began falling out of my first memory,
the ocean above us, one at a time, to get to the bottom of things.

Warm in laughter, easy in tears, steeped in affection, excited to see
my friend, squaring up, air clearing, nothing off limits, as each block
fell into place. That day we rounded the corners, Steve and me. Set to
cut the cord. 100%.

Rocket ship.

What I Learned, This Time Around

In writing this book, there were plenty of times I got carried away explaining what to me was mind-bending/-mending information. I wanted to share every golden moment, every discovery, every chance encounter, every joy that grew out of the muck and the mire.

An awareness of other life forms led to an awareness of people who channel collective beings consciously, co-creating life's experiences, which led me to finding a gift called the Akashic Records, through which other channelers are able to access everything encoded in the ether. That led to remote viewing (introduced to me by an ex-girlfriend from high school, Tiffany Hill, who also volunteered that she had been abducted), holographs, vantage points, dimensions and all the other *Which Ones?* who live in them. All of it led me to take a metaphysics class that led to notebooks filled with the inspiration caused by new information in alignment with my experiences and highest ideals.

That last paragraph will have to make up for the forty pages we cut in order to keep this reading experience manageable. I found myself too closely mining the details and baggage of events, which shifted my mindset from the love I was learning to the exhaustion that causes defensiveness. It's a dead-end job convincing people who live on the other side of my assumptions that my experiences are true, instead of just presenting the experiences as confirmation of what others may already know is happening.

Craving for people to believe there is a way out of the heaviness is its own heaviness, and it was weighing this book down. I suspect, in moments, it still does.

The generous editors have helped me thin it all out by the deadlines I keep outliving. There are lyrics I insisted be included, poems that may have more food in their mouths than is considered appropriate for chewing, spoken word pieces better suited to live onstage, and thoughts I was encouraged to not share at all. I insisted some of those things be included. The weird, the self-indulgent, and the brutal are all on me. It is my intention to be a witness, to cause safety in those who may live in dispositions similar to mine, to help give a gritty thing over to light, and to show that no one's alone in this life, weird, self-indulgent, and brutal as it may be.

There is a line of poetry that is always on my radar. It's by Andrea Gibson. More than any other line Andrea has ever spoken, there is the one I wanna listen to in every language, scored in every genre of every medium. It's a line from the poem "Birthday," and it goes like this:

I suppose I love this life.

I suppose I do.

I suppose the opportunity to live this life is equal to the responsibility to investigate it. I hope my small contributions pair well with all the other fingers doing their best to point us in the right direction, and right on time.

On March 26, 2016, I was in the bathtub finishing *A New Earth* by Eckhart Tolle after eight months of reading it in tiny digestible doses:

So when you become aligned with the whole, you become a conscious part of the interconnectedness of the whole and its purpose: the emergence of consciousness into this world. As a result, spontaneous helpful occurrences, chance encounters, coincidences, and synchronistic events happen much more frequently. Carl Jung called synchronicity an acausal connecting principle. This means there is no causal connection between synchronistic events on our surface level of reality.

100-percenter Derrick Brown taught me, *The worst thing you have ever been through has always been a fair fight.* If we really are all one, as a reality, not as a concept, it is impossible for this line of poetry to be false.

I learned that what happened in childhood wasn't personal. I've learned how to better live than survive, by not having a mouthful of answers, by remembering to listen, and to watch, and to locate the space in everything.

I learned how to stop living in the illusion that I'll lose everything if I suspend my narrative, my identity, the story of it. I learned how immensely intimidated I've been to want love, because what was originally presented to me as love is, in fact, embarrassing. I learned how the blockages I've had against pure love, and the ephemeral comfort I found by burrowing into those blockages, made it extraordinarily difficult for me to hear the positive forces wanting to communicate a better life (in the same way humans deeply wish for our sick animals to know when we are doing everything in our power to ease their suffering).

I learned that devastation has been easy to find in common with others. I learned to understand the network of lives playing into our capabilities, and the politics in play as well. I learned to walk with those who are moving from dark to light, and from light to light. I learned that humans are the masters of limitation. I learned that there are people working diligently to control the idea of safety. I learned that if good people want to help right our listing political ship, those good people must want change more than those who crave power. Those who crave power are too often driven by the intoxicating, unfortunate disposition of ill will. I learned that it's okay to start again. I also learned to be a details man, but to not give every detail away.

I learned that surrendering doesn't mean controlling what happens next. I learned that *Now* is all that ever was or will be, and I wish the philosophy majors spending all that money on their education would know that answer as enough, then save up for a nice camper van, or foster a child instead. I learned that a theory can be disproven, but that which is experiential can only be disbelieved. I learned that being believed or disbelieved for my experience chooses my friends for me.

I learned a meditation practice that keeps this body in check, keeps its chemistry from shifting, and making a muddy swamp of what's important. I learned *Don't wait*. I learned *Don't weight*. I learned about location frequency, how electricity moves faster than dead animals and pizza dough. I learned that telepathic communication is normal, the way cell phones are normal, that the reception improves when I'm not distracted by every anxious endeavor. It improves the most when I'm celibate. I learned what it means to be taken by an alien without the need for windows or doors. I learned that serendipity is my superpower, and despite its fluffy name, it is mine to own.

I learned to not call my highest ideals *unrealistic*.
I learned that, while I haven't always felt a sense of worth,
I have always felt purpose. I learned that having a strong sense of
purpose probably nails a couple bullet points on the narcissist's
checklist, so it is crucial that I handle purpose with care. Luckily, I'm
obsessed with doing my best. I learned that *best* has no ceiling, and
that *balance* is what was meant when I first heard the word *perfection*. I
learned that balance includes the epic fails necessary to
teach me both.

I learned about making the lightest, most exciting
choices, and with zero expectations of the outcome.
I learned how to no longer use all my wounds as
evidence of unworthiness, that instigating my own
trauma was the lowest I could sink.

I learned that nice guys may finish last, but they do finish,
and there's no guarantee finishing first makes a person any happier.

I learned that we live happily ever after we stop avoiding right now.

God is everything happening at once.

—**The Moment**, with regards to itself

Riled Up and Wasted on Light

You remember that time
we sat on top of the whole world
and told each other jokes about the ocean,
until everybody crumbled
into tattoos
of bakeries?

It smelled good.
Felt right.
We laughed
so much. That night
you wore a banana croissant and chocolate waders.
We were looking for a four-leaf clover.
It had nothing to do with luck. Any revelation.
Any size. If we thought it would help,
we would give it to you
like a drunk octopus
riled up and wasted on light

like this, like, *Energy*
can neither be created nor destroyed. That means
we are all exactly the same age, happening at exactly the
same time. Well well welcome
to a room full of self-declared *old souls*
in juvenile clothes.
Let's blow the cake off our candles
and the starving off the words
that are stuck to our throats.

Hello
everybody.

Goodbye
everybody.

Dear Everybody,
do this:

Pretend we are on an airplane now
because we are
and that the cabin is undergoing rapid decompression
because it is
and that the oxygen masks have dropped
because they have.

The adults (that's you)
now get about fifteen to twenty seconds
of useful consciousness
to help themselves
so they can help the children
at thirty-nine thousand feet in the clouds, y'all, listen—

We can stick anything into the fog
and make it look like a ghost.
But tonight
let us not become tragedies.
We are not funeral homes
with propane tanks in our windows
looking like cemeteries.
Cemeteries
are just the Earth's way of not letting go.
Let go.

Tonight,
let's turn our ridiculous wrists
so far backwards
that the razor blades in our pencil tips
can't get a good angle on all that beauty inside.
Step into this
with your airplane parts. Move forward
and repeat after me with your heart:

I no longer need you to fuck me as hard as I hated myself.

Make love to me
like you know I am better
than the worst thing I ever did.
Go slow. I'm new to this.

But I have seen nearly every city in the world
from a rooftop
without jumping. I have realized
that the moon
did not have to be full for us to love it,
that we are not tragedies stranded here beneath it,
that if my heart
really broke
every time I fell from love
I'd be able to offer you confetti by now.

But hearts don't break, y'all, they bruise and get better.
We were never tragedies. We were emergencies.
Go ahead, call 9-1-1.
Tell them I'm having a fantastic time.

Tell them I am right here
right now, with you
at the mouth. *This* is my church.
And if church is a house of healing, *Hallelujah!*
Welcome! Come on in
as you are. Have a look around. Stay out of my porn.

There are massive stacks of bad choices in my backyard.
Clearly, I have not yet reached enlightenment
beyond a few fleeting moments,
but I'm trying, and I found something
here I want you to have.
It ain't much. It's just a story, but it's all I've got.
So take it,

and ask them
when you're talking to them
(because I know some of you tragedy addicts
are all the time talking to them, 9-1-1), ask them, *Hey!?*

Do you remember that time we dressed up like electric
whales and we wrote out the sheet music to green lights
using elephant engine kite string
strong enough to fly this ticking time machine
right up and out of the gospels of our junkyard ghost?

Well, we do. It went beautifully.
We thanked goodness
just enough. That day
filled the black hole in our chest
with breath
and we were cooled in the jets, and we were
kept in the head, and to the people we love
we calmly said:

Yes, you are the center of the universe.
If you weren't you wouldn't be here.
So, as the middle of space, and everything floating in it,
it is your job to know that the emptiness
is just emptiness. And the stars
are just stars. And the flying rocks
fucking hurt. So, please,

stop inviting walls into wide-open spaces.
I know everything is out there.
That's why they call it *everything.*
I know there are times
you will lay your head to rest,
you'll have a moment of brilliance
that grows into a perfect order of words
but you will fall asleep
instead of painting it down on paper.

When you wake up
you will have forgotten the idea completely
and miss it like a front tooth,
but at least you know how to recognize moments of
brilliance
because even at your worst
you are fucking incredible.
It comes honest.

So return to yourself
even if you're already there
because no matter *where* you go,
or how hard you try,
or what you do, the only person you are ever gonna
get to be, and I know it, thank God
God
God
is you.

So yeah if *you*
came here tonight
worn out from the day or the week
or your life, or the voice in your head making the
same arguments, over and over and over again
to no end to make sure
you're the one who's right,
all your defenses,
wearing a deeper groove with each rotation,
the suffering,

then for the rest of this poem,
or the rest of your life,
your choice,
please ask it to have a seat next to you.

And let it go.

Let go let God let it go.
Leave it alone.
Let it pass.
Let it be.
C'est la vie.
Laissez-faire.
What's done is done. Hang up on it.
Land the plane.
Don't get on that train.
The bus has already left.
This too shall pass.
Shake it off.
Cut your losses.
Bust loose. Break free.
It's water under the bridge.
What comes around goes around.
Go around.
Get over it.
Get it together.
Get a grip.
Get moving.
Keep moving.
Move on. Move forward.
Forward. March.
Stop it. Drop it. Squash it.
Please. Release. Relax.
Spilled water cannot be poured back.
Do not look back.
Enough is enough.
Stand down. Stay still.
Be quiet. Yield. Quit dwelling.
Forget it. Forgive it. Right now. As is.
You will be given back
the years that the locusts have taken.
Nothing is against us.
Our cravings for annihilation
will be laid to rest
with the apocalyptic resentment
and the compounding stress

and *Yes*, said the answer,
Yes, said the breath,
The consequences are immediate,
so when you breathe
you might try freeing both lungs up.

Investigate.

—**Magic**, giving away the secret

In Good Company: The Acknowledgments

Nearly every family member mentioned in "Farmly" now has children of their own, especially Morgan, who manages six. All hail. Those kids are the stars of the short film, *Farmly*, shot in 2017 and directed by my friend, Jamie DeWolf. It won the Texas Award at the USA Film Festival, and won Best in Texas at the Literally Short Film Fest in Houston. It's to be released at the end of 2019. Everyone in the film is family. The last shot is my pride and joy. It is a beautiful thing, the span of us.

They've been tremendously generous and hands-off in letting me unpack my life experience publicly, even when it includes them in unpleasant lights. They've allowed me to express and use my voice without being ashamed of how aggressively I've done so. Everyone mentioned in the poem "Farmly" deserves praise for not asking that I adjust my experience to make us look better than how it actually played out from my perspective. They've allowed me to stare shame in the face, without interrupting. When I stare shame in the face it scurries apart.

When *Farmly* proved too intense to screen for the young ones, I wrote "We Are in the Snack!" so I'd be able to simply edit a bunch of footage of them playing, slap some great music to it, then let them watch themselves. "We Are in the Snack!" is also for my nephew, Liam, who lets me call him boogers or poop or jelly donut barf brain breath. Because it makes us laugh. Why wouldn't it? I had no idea when I set out to write this poem that it would give me as much joy as it has.

I know I've done something profoundly right with my life when I have a look at the people with whom I surround myself. This book exists with tremendous love and thanks for:

Kaylen Alan Krebsbach My tour manager on the U.S. legs of the Riled Up and Wasted on Light World Tour (Skipping Chechnya). For sharing your life, youth, humor, talent and patience, bearing witness to how overwhelming it got, and still being my friend. Your commitment was a show of the trust and resilience I hope you will always have for yourself as well. I don't know many people, let alone wild and wide-eyed 19-year-old rulers of the world, who could have brought to the table the wherewithal that you and Uncle Ricky's Husband found for me. The Steel Horse. Our Silver Stallion. The highway lines we had to laugh out of us. Plump when ya cook'm.

Andrea Gibson My room when I finally came home. My room even after I left. All the rooms in England. For the unspeakable risk. For writing a love poem about me on the day I made you maddest. I love you so much I would tackle you to the ground every time I see you if I didn't think you are the answer to "Why are we here?" and because I am scared I would break you in half, you every friend anybody ever wanted, my air traffic control, my sweet forever Faye.

Cristin O'Keefe Aptowicz Would give any lover of life in the world the words that keep her back straight if she thought you'd get a good poem out of it, or if it would cause you success in any way. The warmest hug on Earth. Her epic poem is already written, and I am thankful success has welcomed her home.

Bret Turner Much was deleted from this book in the editing process for the sake of everybody's wellbeing. Among those deletions was a funny memory about Bret and salvia divinorum. In writing about Bret, I reminisced over the unrestrained laughter of him, of the junior high and high school lives we lived together. I remember the startling possibility of a genius in our drugs, and the astronaut wit of the people we ran with, their aggressive exploration of not-limitation, the dissident humor, belonging. What a privilege to have kept a lifelong friendship with the fearless hysterical audacity of you, Bret, even from a distance, and all that perseverance driving your golden heart to be better.

For years, decades with some, I dropped out of contact with my teenage friends after coming out. I'm often considerate to a fault. I didn't want any of them to have to carry the weight of everyone from our hometown wondering if they'd gotten gay with me. I didn't want anyone to question how authentic my friendships were, or if I had an agenda in being their friend. There was none. Not even an attraction, beyond what keeps two kids laughing. Even if there had been, I was never the type to test it. To the peers I left behind, that was my issue. I wish I hadn't been scared to tell you in the first place. Growing up gay cost me a lot of things, not the least of which were some of your friendships. I wish I had known you could handle it, or that it wouldn't hurt me if you didn't.

AIR Besienderhuis and Wintertuin, Dennis Gaens, Kim Van Kaam, Jan-Wieger van den Berg, and Corrie Kuijs, for gifting me with ineffable warmth during the winter of the world tour, then letting me come back to continue working even after. Your kindness and efforts are not missed on me. Thank you for the space to create some of my fondest memories and poems, and with the most fun and loyal crew of friends in Europe.

AIR Serenbe Michael Bettis, Brandon Hinman, and Cristin O'Keefe Aptowicz, thank you for affording me the space to focus on this book, and to live a sense of arrival, a point of success.

Leigh Adams and Sarah "InkyMole" Coleman For Council, you gentleman, and the work, you gentlewoman, and the safety. Both of you, 100%. For driving thousands of miles over the last twelve years to tote me around England, tour after tour. The pre-show madness, and the after-show radness. The walks to town. Every single town. The pints. The power naps. Empire Fitness. Silchar. The goddamn tea. For bringing the biggest, most accommodating tent you could possibly find. For the camper van. The titling. The Factory Road gallery show. Every artist you gave me. All of the work. Every bit. The detail. The storage. The meals. For offering me the opposite of shame about my mischievous behaviors. Every. Single. Time. For home away from home. And movie night. For every Coleman. And the laughter, the years of it, in pun, and penises. The insight. The tolerance of my worst. The sharing of joy at my best.

Anybody can sympathize with the sufferings of a friend, but it requires a very fine nature to sympathize with a friend's success.
—Oscar Wilde

Thank you for sympathizing with my success. You two are my role models for how it works when it works.

Lane Stroud is a growth junkie, has a crush on bravery and answers to the quit of no one. She teaches me in "obviouslies," like the fact that I must chew carefully because there is a passive aggressive monster who still lives in at least two of the 28 teeth I use to bite apples. *I am glad you're not an asshole*, Lane said, *because you would be a good one.* Lane Stroud caused the year of the rain to stop. *Somebody call the sky and tell them it's summer.* I woke up around you. For every time in this book I mentioned the danger of having a mouthful of answers, Lane taught me that. She is half of the first screenplay I ever wrote. The grounded half.

Danny Sherrard is his own relay race to the light, a one-man celebration of what's possible just before possible happens, but he still doesn't remember how he ended up with Mick Jagger's mojo. Watching him perform poetry is like watching professional double Dutch jumpers juggle goose bumps with the ropes on fire. It's fun for Danny to see people reach for the stars. It's where he lives. Loves visitors. Go go go.

CJ Leavens Every cell of you, woman. Your name and the word *Hallelujah* feel synonymous. Because of you I fear no black hole or Mariana Trench. Thank you for coming over with all that clarity. All that light. The night you showed up when my life depended on it. For all the judgments you suspended or expelled and cleared and made gone. For the Akashic Records. CJ is pivotal to me giving the most self-love ever given. Regarding Akashic readings, please feel comfortable contacting cjleavens@gmail.com. Tell her I sent you.

Carl Hornibrook Every step. The Basement. The Sydney Opera House. For letting me rest. Your patience and generosity. The guardrails. The sailing. For going to the airport to pick up the lost books while I slept. Yosemite. The hot spring. For driving the ambulance down the coast after Folsom. Hawaii. The care. All the detail in the care. You have made a safe transfer of me, Carl. And a better man of me. In the keenest of ways. If you were a gratitude tax collector, I would not be able to afford the thanks I owe you. But I'll try: Thank you, Carl. o

Stephen Snook reminded me it is not necessary to trust others with what I can trust myself to do well. Expectations of others are the swinging gates to resentment. I was an angry saloon. I don't even like to gunfight. I had so many expectations that weren't fair to you while you were accepting me for who I was. Thank you for accepting me for who I am, even still. For the ways you made me feel safe. And for all three books you lived through with me.

When I took his hand in mine, for a little while, everything was alright.
—**Perfume Genius**

Lace Williams Cousin, I can't imagine any life without you in it. Please come to all of them.

Derrick C. Brown Oh brother.

Tresa B. Olsen Oh Mom.

For bearing witness when it counted most: Ani DiFranco, Oliver Klomp, Paul Anka, Helen Vonderheide, Heather Mann, Megan Falley, Emily Clay, Bruce Tift, Julie Colwell, David Olsen, Jeffrey Olsen, Shelly Horelica, Perry Sjogren, AJ Whipple, Jenny Whipple, Steve Noble, Seth Terrell, Taalam Acey, Shihan Van Clief, Denise Jolly, Tiffany Woody Hill, Ashlee Haze, Inkera Oshun, Alex Krispin, Laney Williams, Timmy Straw, Emily Wells, Sascha Lewis, Joe Kowalke, Stephen Bowden, Jon & Sherri Berardi, Jessica Berardi, Aldo Valdez, Lizzy Ellison, Brendan Constantine, Danielle Plunkett, Jonathan Drew Johnson, Shona Strausser, John Kim, Amber Tamblyn, David Cross, Tasha Blank, Dogger, Remond Liesting, Clay Davidson, Emily Pennington, Alex Polinski, Norman Lear, Alexander Gould,

Judith Kinitz, Kim van Kaam, Eline van Wieren, Lotte Lentes, Juliet Gagnon, David O'Dowda, Dulcie Whitman, Niek Groven, Nena Tijsma, niekennena.nl, Nas Dean, Matthew Earthspirit, Alan Sereboff, Thuli Zuma & Nkululeko Page Ngwenya, Milana Vayntrub, Dr. Afua Cooper, Tanya Evanson, Nardean, Andy Deck, Sarah Healy, Sara Boulter, Brock Stapper, Lexi Miller-Golub, Todd Sickafoose, Ilana Umansky, Jon Ryan Sugimoto, Amanda Rafkin, Mike Roff, Patricia Kucmanova, Derek McGhee and his family, Jeremy Radin. Sandy, James and Liam Roach. Ryan, Jayce, Rhett, Tate, Abigail, Angel, Eric and Morgan Alms. The Hensons, Summer Whitmore, Scott Woods, Anna Freeman, Keaton Maddox, Alyesha Wise, Tonya Ingram, Matthew Cuban, Veronika Shulman, Roger Bonair-Agard, Lynne Procope, Pieter Vodden, Jeff Scarborough, Tyler Manzo, Alejandro Cardenas, Camille Carida, Sonya Renee Taylor, Lino Anunciacion, Ed Voccola, Max Kessler, Travis Tohill, Benny Pearson, Jared Webber, Bret & Maria Morris, the ongoing bravery of Dylan, and Bryan Medina. And anyone else who knows they should be on this list.

Chad Turner, Tim Sanders, Steve Snook, and Jason Byron Nelson for their talent, time and effort helping me to arrive at the perfect cover for this book.

Roger Ballen for his generosity in accepting way less than the billion bucks he's worth. Go see why at rogerballen.com

Write Bloody Publishing, Aly Sarafa, and Aaron Silverman for giving me way past the deadline to hand in exactly the cover (and poems) I wanted for this book. For your untold help along the way and ahead.

For **Laurel & Hardy**, who introduced joy to my world.

Neither Mr. Laurel nor Mr. Hardy had any thoughts of doing wrong. As a matter of fact, they had no thoughts of any kind.
—**Stan Laurel**, *The Hoose-Gow* (1929)

S.N. Goenka and Vipassana centers around the world for showing me that gratitude is best expressed by showing up, not in saying it.

Vipassana sleeping quarters and every delicious vegetarian meal are provided with love by volunteers at well-equipped, exceptionally maintained centers around the world. If you ever wish to register for a Vipassana course and someone tries to charge you money, you're in the wrong place. Dhamma.org.

Eckhart Tolle has obviously had a huge impact on my life. I wish the words "Thank you" hadn't been invented yet so I could say them for the first time right now. The first "Thank you" that ever entered the world must've just been a big fat smile.

NOTES AND CREDITS

All **ECKHART TOLLE** quotes are from *The Power of Now* and *A New Earth*.

SONYA RENEE's insight in "On 12/28/13" is from a conversation we had on Facebook.

SCOTT WOODS' remarks in "On 12/28/13" are from a post he made to Facebook.

RICHARD GERE's speech in "The Gift of My Hate" is truncated. You did great.

The **PIXAR** movie *Inside Out* is responsible for the line "Anger is only concerned with what it thinks is fair," in the poem "The Gift of My Hate." The original line is "That's Anger. He cares very deeply about things being fair."

The original version of **"The Gospel of Lightning"** is nearly nine minutes long, and far more specific to the bride and groom. It can be found on YouTube.

CJ LEAVENS inspired the line involving "...obligated to love" in "Heret Herot." CJ is also responsible for most of the answer in "Before Fealty."

Googling "Heret Herot" yielded a **WIKIPEDIA** result, from which the Beowulf explanation was quoted to bits.

MAYA ANGELOU's quote, "When someone shows you who they are, believe them the first time" directly inspired the line, "When someone tells you they love you, believe them," in "Heret Herot."

STEFANY COCA (@fragile.bird.bones on Instagram) sent the clarifying quote about the wet snake trying to become an octopus in "Armageddon with Mom."

ANDREA GIBSON's line, "I suppose I love this life" is from the poem "Birthday" from the book *Pole Dancing to Gospel Hymns* (Write Bloody Publishing, 2008).

DERRICK C. BROWN's line, "The worst thing you have ever been through has always been a fair fight." is from "Church of the Broken Axe Handle," from the book *Uh-Oh* (Write Bloody Publishing, 2016).

HELEN VONDERHEIDE showed me the concept of using wounds as evidence of unworthiness, included in "What I Learned, This Time Around."

BASHAR, as channeled by Paul Anka, is the inspiring source for a passage in "What I Learned, This Time Around;" Bashar's original quote being, "Follow your highest excitement with zero, and I mean ZERO, expectations of the outcome."

"Riled Up and Wasted on Light" combines a few previously published poems from the book *Stunt Water* (Write Bloody Publishing, 2015), alongside new material that demands their company. Excerpts in order are: "We Were Emergencies," "Human the Death Dance," "The Information Man," and "Let It Go."

A clever mind is not a heart.
　　—**Benjamin Hoff**, *The Tao of Pooh*
That quote is not at all referenced in this book. But if it ever is, now you know.

ALL NAMES have been kept true where possible.

ANYONE written about in this book, among the weightier, more incriminating subject matter, has granted full permission for me to use their name, except Jimmy Morin.

About the Author

BUDDY WAKEFIELD was the first author released on Write Bloody Publishing. He is a three-time world champion spoken word artist, and the most toured performance poet in history. He now lives in Los Angeles, CA, as a free agent pursuing acting and screenwriting for both television and film.

www.buddywakefield.com

Epilogue

Wakefield is the last name I chose.
Pulled it from a song without overthinking.
Beasley was the last name I was born with.
My friend Leigh loves etymology and looked it up.
Beasley means *bent grass in a clearing*.
The name was first found in Warwickshire,
thirty minutes down the road from Leigh's house.
The first official record of the name appears to be of one
Gracia Beesley, on a church document,
stating that she married William Wackfield.

IF YOU LIKE BUDDY WAKEFIELD, BUDDY LIKES...

Birthday Girl with Possum
Brendan Constantine

Slow Dance with Sasquatch
Jeremy Radin

Open Your Mouth Like a Bell
Mindy Nettifee

Drive Here and Devastate Me
Megan Falley

Pole Dancing to Gospel Hymns
Andrea Gibson

Write Bloody Publishing publishes and promotes great books of poetry every year. We believe that poetry can change the world for the better. We are an independent press dedicated to quality literature and book design, with an office in Los Angeles, California.

We are grassroots, DIY, bootstrap believers. Pull up a good book and join the family. Support independent authors, artists, and presses.

Want to know more about Write Bloody books, authors, and events? Join our mailing list at

www.writebloody.com

WRITE BLOODY BOOKS

After the Witch Hunt — Megan Falley

Aim for the Head: An Anthology of Zombie Poetry — Rob Sturma, Editor

Amulet — Jason Bayani

Any Psalm You Want — Khary Jackson

Atrophy — Jackson Burgess

Birthday Girl with Possum — Brendan Constantine

The Bones Below — Sierra DeMulder

Born in the Year of the Butterfly Knife — Derrick C. Brown

Bouquet of Red Flags — Taylor Mali

Bring Down the Chandeliers — Tara Hardy

Ceremony for the Choking Ghost — Karen Finneyfrock

A Choir of Honest Killers — Buddy Wakefield

A Constellation of Half-Lives — Seema Reza

Counting Descent — Clint Smith

Courage: Daring Poems for Gutsy Girls — Karen Finneyfrock,
Mindy Nettifee, & Rachel McKibbens, Editors

Dear Future Boyfriend — Cristin O'Keefe Aptowicz

Do Not Bring Him Water — Caitlin Scarano

Don't Smell the Floss — Matty Byloos

Drive Here and Devastate Me — Megan Falley

Drunks and Other Poems of Recovery — Jack McCarthy

The Elephant Engine High Dive Revival — Derrick C. Brown, Editor

Everyone I Love Is a Stranger to Someone — Annelyse Gelman

Everything Is Everything — Cristin O'Keefe Aptowicz

Favorite Daughter — Nancy Huang

The Feather Room — Anis Mojgani

Floating, Brilliant, Gone — Franny Choi

Glitter in the Blood: A Poet's Manifesto for Better, Braver Writing — Mindy Nettifee

Gold That Frames the Mirror — Brandon Melendez